"This inspiring book tells the remarkable stor
one of the world's leading nonviolent educators
geous and dedicated staff member of the Soutnern Christian ....
Conference, working closely with my father, Dr. Martin Luther King Jr.
*The Life of Harcourt Klinefelter Peace Apostle: Globalizing the Dream of Dr.
Martin Luther King Jr.* provides an important contribution to the history
of the movement, an invaluable resource for learning about the civil rights
movement from an insider perspective and for exploring creative ways to
build diverse nonviolent movements for social and economic justice in the
future."
—Martin Luther King III

"Rev. Harcourt Klinefelter is a legend. He's one of the most fascinating people I've ever met. I could have listened to his stories for hours . . . and now, thanks to this book, we actually can. It's true that our best sermon is our life. And the life of Harky Klinefelter is among the best sermons I've ever heard."
—Shane Claiborne
author and activist

"Nonviolence liberates, if you work with others! The convincing proof of this reality is found in real life of real communities in real conflicts. And it is best witnessed in biographies of individuals, whose faith provided the calling, the courage, and the spiritual resources to walk such a way of life. Rev. Harcourt Klinefelter is a most telling and encouraging example."
—Fernando Enns
Vrije Universiteit Amsterdam

"Harcourt Klinefelter has spent a lifetime dedicated to teaching and following in daily life Christ's call to nonviolence, justice, and reconciliation. His years of serving with Dr. Martin Luther King Jr. give him a unique perspective on one of the most significant nonviolent struggles for social justice witnessed in human history. Since that time, he has been faithfully implementing the teachings of Dr. King—as grounded in the teachings of Jesus Christ—in his role as a minister and strong advocate for nonviolence in confronting injustice and the precipitous march to war."
—Richard Blackburn
Executive Director, Lombard Mennonite Peace Center, Illinois

"Harcourt Klinefelter's life and witness give evidence that he is a contemporary peace apostle in like manner as Dr. Martin Luther King Jr."
—**Elizabeth A. Raid**
    pastor, writer, pilgrim for peace

"This biography of Klinefelter gives the reader three valuable experiences: insight into the culture of the United States in the fascinating 60s and 70s, a surprising picture of the varied work of Harky Klinefelter, and a source of inspiration for everyone who seeks courage to stand up in the world today and work for justice and peace. Whoever reads this book experiences something of what Jesus said: 'Blessed are the peacemakers.'"
—**Ciska Stark**
    Protestant Theological University in Amsterdam and Groningen

The Life
of
Peace Apostle
Harcourt Klinefelter

The Life of Peace Apostle Harcourt Klinefelter

Globalizing the Dream
of
DR. MARTIN LUTHER KING JR.

HARCOURT KLINEFELTER
Foreword by *Andrew J. Young*

WIPF & STOCK · Eugene, Oregon

THE LIFE OF PEACE APOSTLE HARCOURT KLINEFELTER
Globalizing the Dream of Dr. Martin Luther King

Copyright © 2019 Harcourt Klinefelter. All rights reserved. Except for brief quotations in critical publications or reviews, no part of this book may be reproduced in any manner without prior written permission from the publisher. Write: Permissions, Wipf and Stock Publishers, 199 W. 8th Ave., Suite 3, Eugene, OR 97401.

Wipf & Stock
An Imprint of Wipf and Stock Publishers
199 W. 8th Ave., Suite 3
Eugene, OR 97401

www.wipfandstock.com

PAPERBACK ISBN: 978-1-5326-6501-1
HARDCOVER ISBN: 978-1-5326-6502-8
EBOOK ISBN: 978-1-5326-6503-5

Manufactured in the U.S.A.   OCTOBER 10, 2019

Mrs. Katrien Ruitenburg and Narratio gave permission to use the Dutch version as base for the English version without copy right.

Original title: Het leven van vredesapostel Harcourt Klinefelter
Sub title: Globalisering van de droom van Dr. Martin Luther King
Writer: Mrs. Katrien Ruitenburg
Translator: mrs. Betty Lavooy
Dutch ISBN: 978 90 5263 9383
NUR: 707

2018 theologische uitgeverij Narratio
www.harcourt-klinefelter.org

Contents

Foreword by Andrew J. Young | vii
Preface | xiii

1. I Am Darker Than You | 1
2. Never Expected and Yet Fulfilled | 15
3. At the Side of Dr. Martin Luther King, Jr. | 28
4. The Street Has Many Faces | 45
5. A Lifetime of Learning | 62
6. Standing Side by Side | 84
7. Working for Peace across Borders | 102
8. Raising Courageous Citizens | 123
9. You Can Kill the Dreamer, but Not the Dream | 153

Words of Thanks | 173
Appendix A—Principles of Nonviolence | 175
Appendix B—Résumé | 192
Appendix C—Photo and poem credits | 197

Foreword

WHEN REV. KLINEFELTER ASKED me to write the foreword to this book, I was very happy to do this for my friend.

Harky is an extraordinary person with many talents. He is a minister of the Gospel, an adult educator, a peace theologian, mediator, nonviolent trainer, activist, and an audio technician, among other things.

Atlanta and the US

I got to know Harky and later his Dutch wife when we worked together in the *Southern Christian Leadership Conference* (SCLC). We were together at

Foreword

conventions, staff retreats, demonstrations and informal parties. After he moved to the Netherlands, we continued to have contact. Over the years I met with him when I went to the Netherlands and a number of times in Atlanta, Georgia.

I first met Harky when he came to Selma, Alabama in the spring of 1965. This was during the Voter Rights Campaign. He was a student in Yale Divinity School and came as a volunteer. He had a portable tape recorder with him. In those days it was something quite unique. He began to record events that the media had missed. He sent the actualities over the telephone to radio and television stations. After the famous march from Selma to Montgomery, he interviewed local residents who marched the whole way.

Harky returned in the summer for the *Summer Community Organizing and Political Education Program* (SCOPE) voter-register program. During the training session led by Bayard Rustin, he was able to use his technical abilities to enhance the program by making it possible to listen to the speakers on the participant's portable radios. At the end of the summer, he was asked to join the staff as Assistant Director of Public Relations and Media Director. Dr. Martin Luther King asked Yale Divinity School to grant him an internship. This was later extended for another year. In this capacity he was responsible, among other things, for making the tape recordings of Dr. King's speeches and sermons as well as other newsworthy events. Dr. King entrusted him to edit them into radio programs which were sent out over 300 stations for over several decades.

That summer he met Annelies Koopmans, who came as a Dutch exchange visitor with the Mennonite Church, and a romance began, but after a year her visa was up. She returned to the Netherlands. The only way to get her back was to get married in the Netherlands, which Harky did in December 1966.

After two years working with SCLC, Dr. King advised Harky that he should return to Yale Divinity School and finish his last year of study now, otherwise he would never do it. Reluctantly he did so. There he continued his activities that he began in Atlanta in the anti-war movement. He led demonstrations in New Haven, Connecticut. He risked five years in jail when he, not once but twice, turned in his draft card as a protest.

He used SCLC as an example in his thesis: *The Church as a Movement Rather than an Institute*.

Shortly before Harky would finish his Master of Divinity Degree, Dr. King was assassinated. Harky flew to Atlanta the next day. Harky was responsible for the media coverage of the funeral. He made it possible for an excerpt of the sermon in which Dr. King said what he wanted told at his funeral to be played. The whole world heard this.

Upon finishing his degree, Harky returned to SCLC and was the liaison between the National Council of Churches and Resurrection City, the tent city protest on the Mall in Washington, DC, that was part of the Poor People's Campaign. This campaign brought Afro-Americans, poor Whites, Native Americans, Hispanics and other minorities together to demand a guaranteed annual income.

The following year he was ordained as a minister in the United Church of Christ (Congregationalist). Dr. Martin Luther King Sr., "Daddy King," preached the sermon in Harky's hometown church in Glen Ridge, New Jersey, at this ordination.

Later that year the SCLC ran out of money, and Harky and many others were laid off.

At that time Atlanta was becoming a hippie center. He began helping hippies from out of his house. Every day there were half a dozen hippies at the dinner table; persons who needed special help slept in his study. The United Church of Christ, the Disciples of Christ and the United Presbyterians funded the program, *The Ministry to the Street People*. "Reverend Harky" was responsible for setting up many projects and was especially active helping run-away teenagers.

(The letter of recommendation I wrote for this project is in Chapter 4.)

In the midst of this, his first child, Thea Lucia, was born.

Although Harky's work with hippies was planned for three years, after two years the money dried up.

Dr. King saw war, racism and poverty as being intrinsically interconnected. Harky was deeply involved in the peace movement in Atlanta, George, New Haven, Connecticut and in Washington, D.C. May Day, 1971, was the high point of the protests against the war in Vietnam. Harky trained and led demonstrations in the largest civil disobedience campaign in which 10,000s participated in sit-ins in Washington, DC.

Europe

Harky moved to the Netherlands in 1972. He had studied earlier for a year in the University of London. He hoped to further his study, but he ended up working on the production line in a Dutch factory for two years to support his family. Then he worked as an adult educator for a dozen years in a residential adult education center doing consciousness-raising and values-consideration courses. Among other things, he organized and led the first national and international nonviolent training courses in the Netherlands and elsewhere in Europe.

He quickly learned that you cannot just import techniques from one culture into another.

You first need to understand both cultures before you can translate the ideas and techniques.

It was Harky's greatest dream to be able to globalize Dr. King's message. In Europe he was able to do this in many important ways that would most likely not have been so successful had he remained in the USA. In Europe as one of the very few persons who knew Dr. King personally, he was often interviewed by newspapers, magazines, and radio and television stations. He lectured in universities and other schools in the Netherlands, Germany and Ireland. He did non-violent training and mediation courses in Sweden, Denmark, Belgium and other countries as well as during the war in Ex-Yugoslavia in Serbia, Croatia and Bosnia. He spoke at national and local demonstrations.

Harky was on the steering committee of international peace groups.

For five years he was the minister of a church. After this period of ministry, Harky was responsible for setting up and giving courses in coping with aggression in refugee centers in the Netherlands. A special foundation was set up so he could do this work. He and his wife went recently with the Christian Peacemaker Teams to work with refugees in Lesbos in Greece.

These are just a few of his activities for peace, freedom and justice. You can read more about these in the book.

What kind of person is Harky?

I believe the following incident gives a good indication of his character.

During the March Against Fear in 1966 Dr. King went into Philadelphia Mississippi where, two years earlier, three Civil Rights workers were murdered. After he spoke an angry mob attacked the marchers. We were out-numbered ten to one. We feared for our lives and tried to march away. An elderly man had an epileptic attack. Harky went directly over to help him. A white nurse came to help. This meant that the attention of the crowd went to them, and the marchers were able to get away to safety. I remember saying, "Goodbye" to him. Not, "I will see you later."

He was part of a group of nonviolent activists who offered to take the place of the hostages when a train was kidnapped by freedom fighters in the Netherlands.

He risked his life to do trainings in Ex-Yugoslavia during the war there.

Why the book is important

Dr. King said in his book, *Why We Can't Wait*, "In measuring the whole implications of the civil-rights revolution, the greatest contribution may be in the area of world peace. . . . Nonviolence, the answer to the Negro's need, may become the answer to the most desperate need of all humanity."

Here lies the reason this book is so significant. Harky as no other has spent his life promoting Dr. King's dream of globalizing nonviolent social change not only in the Netherlands where he lives, but throughout Europe.

Not only did Harky have technical recording and editing skills as well as theological and philosophical training, he personally knew Dr. King and his family and those about him. This personal relationship gave Harky a unique perspective from which initially to edit Dr. King's sermons and speeches and, later, to speak and write about Dr. King's legacy.

More important is the fact that, although the media constantly emphasize the rhetorical genius of Dr. King, Harky fully grasped what was far more important for posterity: Dr. King's theology, philosophy and techniques of nonviolent social change based on the spirit of love.

Like the four Evangelists in the Bible who recorded and edited the teachings and life of Jesus, Harky has done the same by recording and editing the words of the Prophet of the twentieth century and his disciples. Saint Paul was responsible for bringing the Gospel to the wider world.

Harky moved to the Netherlands where he has been like Saint Paul in promoting the Dream in Europe.

The book of Acts records the travels of Saint Paul and some of his speeches.

This book does the same for Harky. Just as in the book of Acts, there are suspenseful moments. For Harky, these include being in Sarajevo during the war.

Foreword

There are deep insights and inspired thoughts. Humor is there as well. However its historical importance should not be underestimated. Many photos and articles make it attractive.

Peace and Blessings,

[signature: Andrew J. Young]

Andrew J. Young, as Executive Director of the Southern Christian Leadership conference (SCLC), was one of King's colleagues, the first black member of Congress in the South for nearly a century, former Ambassador of the US with the UN and mayor of Atlanta twice.

Preface

"The heart of real nonviolence is the belief that each person is an indispensable part of the cosmos, and that the strongest power in the universe is love".

—Harcourt Klinefelter

You are about to begin reading the life's story of Harcourt (usually called "Harky") Klinefelter. This biography is not written because this person is so interesting and important, but because his ideas are. Harky hopes that as many people as possible, especially the young, will learn of his experiences with nonviolent actions. Harky's story clearly indicates how life looks for a person consequently trying to practice the ideal of nonviolence, driven by his passion to globalize the dream of Dr. Martin Luther King Jr.

Nonviolence forms the theme of this book.

Nonviolence is a technique as well as an attitude of life. It is more than refusing to use violence. It uses positive power to fight conflicts and injustice. Nonviolent tactics can be used by everyone without adhering or belonging to a radical nonviolent life style. But nonviolence as a life style is a good basis for promoting a culture of peace and justice.

All of life's aspects are described in the diverse chapters. The story is written so that it is clear what Harky's motivation, methods and ideals are. It is not without reason that he is called a *Peace Apostle* in the title of the book. This apostle of peace explains, in words and deeds, the importance of nonviolence and repeatedly is capable of inspiring the people with whom he comes in contact. The many anecdotes make it clear that this ideal is not

Preface

meant only for extraordinary individuals, but for everyone who dares to make controversial decisions in daily life.

Anyone who reads how Harky attacks discrimination, poverty, war and environmental problems must feel that he is being addressed personally.

We read about the American society as it was when Harky grew up. An unusual path leads to the university and to Harky's calling. We discover what motivates Harky to go to Selma to join the civil rights movement of Dr. Martin Luther King Jr., how he supports hippies as Reverend Harky and how he protests against the Vietnam war.

He constantly takes risks for a good cause. We see how Harky plays his role on the stage of the seventies and eighties of the twentieth century. We follow him to the Netherlands where the love of his life comes from. Together they have three children. We see how he, as a father, struggles with competing desires and goals.

Partly because of the peace courses that Harky gave to adults in the Dutch Adult Education Center *Overcinge* (*Volkshogeschool*), a trained group of Dutch people demonstrated against atomic weapons and atomic energy, and Harky was there.

We see Harky as a minister, as a conflict mediator and trainer in war-torn former Yugoslavia in the nineties. Around the year 2000 he became more and more active as speaker, writer and trainer, climaxing in the renewed work in conflict areas, presently with the Christian Peacemaker Teams (CPT). His life shows that he remains a press agent and a man of peace in all circumstances.

Here and there in the book are short explanations of the theory and techniques of nonviolent actions in varying situations. For more information be sure to read the appendix on *Principles of Nonviolence*.

Harcourt Klinefelter is a dreamer. He dreams not only of global peace and justice as did his great example, Dr. Martin Luther King Jr., but demonstrates that nonviolence works. His dream of a book about his life has become reality as you hold this book in your hands. He dreams on, dreams of readers who, inspired through his example, will bring nonviolent actions into practice and so help to realize a world of righteousness.

This book is based on a previously published biography of Harcourt Klinefelter written in Dutch by Katrien Ruitenburg, *Het leven van vredesapostel Harcourt Klinefelter: Globalisering de droom van Dr. Martin Luther King* (2018). [*The Life of Peace Apostle Harcourt Klinefelter: Globalizing the dream of Dr. Martin Luther King.*]

— 1 —

I Am Darker Than You

THE NAME HARKY COMES from "Harcourt." His full name is Overton Harcourt Klinefelter, Junior. The nurse who assisted at his birth on March 2, 1938, couldn't believe her ears when she heard this name and said, "I'll come back when the anesthetic wears off."

The Family

But father, Overton Harcourt Klinefelter, Senior (born 1908) and mother, Lucille Amanda Burton Klinefelter (born 1906) were certain. They found that there were many reasons to be proud of the name Harcourt. It had been the surname of Harky's ancestors for many centuries. His grandmother, Belle Harcourt, had no brothers, so the name Harcourt would have ceased to exist after her death. For that reason she added the name Harcourt to her son's first names. They called him "Court." Harcourt Junior would rather have had that name too. It sounds much better, also in Dutch, than Harky, but it was Harky, and it stayed Harky.

In Harky's extensive archives, we can find the biography which Annie Frances Harcourt wrote about her husband, Harky's great-grandfather, Richard Harcourt (1840-1911). She dedicates this book to her children and grandchildren, *". . . so they may learn of their respectable heritage and will pursue the life of him who filled his days with a great determination, good deeds and with Christian activities."*

Richard Harcourt

Richard Harcourt's portrait shows an elegant man in a black jacket with a high collar and double row of buttons. A stiff white collar is just barely visible. Richard Harcourt wears a lorgnette with a cord on the left side which disappears under the collar of the jacket. His profession? Minister! There are also a number of his sermons in the archives. Harky's goal of this book is exactly what Annie Frances Harcourt hoped for: that the readers would take his life as an example, not because he was important as a person, but so that his precious experiences would not be lost.

Ancestry

Harky's great-grandmother, the widow Annie Frances Harcourt, proudly writes that the name Harcourt first appears in the registers of Normandy, France, in 876. In the eleventh century, three of his descendants accompany William the Conqueror to England. From that moment on, the Harcourts are named often in English history, and not only in minor positions. Sir Simon Harcourt (1603-1642) brought help to Dublin in 1642 during the Irish uprising. It cost him his life, but a street bears his name: a beautiful avenue, writes Annie Frances. Harky also has a coat of arms, thanks to his ancestors. Richard Harcourt came to the United States from Ireland about 1860.

If we trace the line of Harcourt's mother's maiden name, Burton, we encounter the Pilgrims. The Pilgrims were the first Europeans who, pursued by religious persecution, sought a new life in the New World. In the USA you are quite important if you can trace your ancestors to the Pilgrims. You are almost of nobility.

There is much less known about Harky's surname, Klinefelter. Probably it is an English version of a German name since Kleinfelders originated in the Rhineland of Germany. About 1850 they went to America and settled in Red Hook, New York. The name Klinefelter appears most commonly in Pennsylvania. During the war Harky was told that his surname was Dutch, but later he heard that it was probably of German origin.

A distant cousin of Harky's father, Harry Klinefelter, was a physician. He discovered the Klinefelter Syndrome, a genetic disorder.

When Harky talks about his family, it mostly concerns his parents or his sister, but also his grandparents. Because of the distances between them in the United States, Harky had little contact with his nieces and nephews as a child. He does have one lively memory of staying with his Uncle Everett and Aunt Eloise in New Jersey. "I was seven. I was sitting in the kitchen and heard on the radio that the atomic bomb had been dropped on Hiroshima."

During the war Harky's father offered to serve, but was rejected. His wife was, of course, very happy, but little Harcourt thought it a shame. He thought soldiers were quite cool!

Harky, "I remember that gasoline was rationed during the war, that people listened to reports on the radio, and that the lead wires that were used to seal the milk bottles were collected to make bullets. Other than that there was not much evidence of the war in our daily life." Harky does remember that he was staying at a friend's house for lunch, at about the age of six, and that the comment was made that children in Europe would be very happy to eat the scorned bread crusts.

Harky's cousin, Harcourt Newman, was stationed in Europe where he worked together with a Dutch interpreter. He came with her as his wife after the war on Thanksgiving Day to our house. They saw the elaborately loaded table and could not believe their eyes. "This is more food than we have seen during the whole winter famine."

Family home Glen Ridge, New Jersey

I Am Darker Than You

Harky's home situation

The family lived in Glen Ridge, a long-stretched-out village of about 5000 inhabitants. It was nice to live there: close to New York and yet out in the country. Harky could see Manhattan and the Empire State Building, and the red neon sign of 666 on the World Trade Center from his bedroom. Glen Ridge is unique in the United States because more than 600 lanterns still worked on gas in 2013.

Harky's parents were upper-middle-class citizens, but that was nothing to be proud of in their home.

According to Harky, his parents did not have strong racial prejudices. Harky was also unaware of racial discrimination occurring in the area in which he grew up. "Behind us lived a black family. I had good contact with the children. They called me Horsecow because they could not pronounce Harcourt." It was strange that the fence between us and the black family was six feet high whereas most fences between houses in Glen Ridge were three feet high. I have no idea why." Harky later asked about this but could not find a suitable answer.

Parents on honeymoon, 1935

Harky's parents each belonged to a different Protestant church: mother was Baptist and father was Methodist. Together they attended the Congregational Church in the village. Harky remembers that his sister, Lynn, was born when he was three years old. "I had a gnome doll made of cloth. When my sister was born, the doll needed a band aid on the stomach, just like my sister's navel band..."

A few more memories come to the surface. He remembers that they never quarreled and that their dog made sure that little Lynn didn't run away by biting her ankles if she ventured too far.

Childhood

Harky has no pleasant memories of the primary school in Glen Ridge. He was often picked on. "Once I was beaten up by Tommy and his gang." He says that children were often bullied at school, but bullying was not considered a big problem in those days.

In primary school Harky had a Catholic and a Jewish friend. That was allowed, but his parents preferred him to have Protestant friends. His mother did not want Harky to be with any one friend too much. He assumes it was for fear of homosexuality, but this was never actually said.

His friend, Trent Smith was a Catholic and Harky went to mass with him. He remembers the beautiful clothing of the priest. He also remembers another occasion, "Trent was not allowed to play American football by his mother because it could be dangerous. One day a player slipped on the slippery floor and glided over the floor like a seal. Trent laughed so hard that he fell off the bench and broke his arm. That was the worst injury of the season."

His teacher wanted him to repeat grade two because she did not think that he could read well enough. Harky's mother took an encyclopedia, *Birds of America*, to school. He could read that better than the simple Alice and Tom stories. Even then Harky was interested in birds. Mentally he was far superior to his peers and had little contact with them. His unstable health condition and his mother's reaction to it only increased the gap. He was often ill and was hospitalized regularly so he missed large parts of schooling. (He suffered from chronic sinus infections). His mother was very protective. Harky always had to be very careful with his head. He was not allowed to dive in a swimming pool and nothing was to hit his head while he was playing.

Family, 1945

Harcourt's sister remembers that her big brother had a preference for non-violent conflict-solving as a child. "If a child from the neighborhood came to us and was annoying, Harcourt would speak to him in a strong voice to stop. If that didn't help, Harcourt sent him away. If that didn't work either, Harcourt would call our mother. Only if there really was no other way, would he use his fists."

Harky recalls his first experience with verbal violence. "The mother of a neighbor girl who was crying said to me that I had hurt her daughter: 'You hurt her feelings.'" He learned from this that you can hurt people with words.

A technical father

The summer of 1946 presented an unforgettable experience in Harky's youth. His great-grand grandfather had worked for Thomas Edison. His father, an engineer in telecommunication, had bought a do-it-self kit to make a television. Harky can still recall the parts strewn all over the oval dining room table. His mother read the instructions. When the TV was finally finished, there was picture but no sound. They watched the American football game, their first television event, and followed the comments on the radio. After the sound was fixed, neighborhood children came to watch television in the afternoons. No one else had a TV. Harky was nine when he heard on television that Gandhi, the nonviolent founder of India was murdered in 1948 by a Hindu extremist. He will never forget that moment.

Some of Harky's father's expressions made a deep impression on him. *"Never start a fight, but if you get into one, you have to finish it. A little knowledge is a dangerous thing."*

A complex mother

Lucille Klinefelter's distorted picture of life probably was partly due to the fact that she was addicted to amphetamines. Originally the pills were prescribed to pep her up so she could take care of her two little children and chronically ill husband. A few years before her death, Harky discovered her addiction. Many things fell into place then. A side effect of amphetamines is paranoia. This is why she would never leave Harky alone with his father.

Harky's mother was hyper-intelligent. She had an IQ of 190. She finished her studies in psychology in no time and did research on hypnosis. "The emphasis on intellectual achievements has shaped my life," Harky says. However the atmosphere at home was completely different than at school. At home reading and discussion were appreciated while at school the goal for boys was to be an "all round kid." For this reason social development received more attention than intellectual development in school. After the Sputnik was launched by Russia in 1957, the climate in school changed drastically. Suddenly much more emphasis was placed on excelling in science and technology.

Lucille Klinefelter studied at a time that equal rights for women were being fought for. It is quite understandable that the compulsory existence of a housewife was very frustrating for her. She had quit her job as head of a primary school when the children were born. Nevertheless, Harky remembers that she often said how important it was to her to be home for the children. And she was always there.

Free time

Despite the emphasis on intellectual formation and the protective attitude of his mother, Harky had time to develop himself in sports. When he was ten he learned horseback riding. When he was eleven he went to summer camp for the first time. It was an expensive camp which was supposed to last six weeks. The sports activities were wonderful: horseback riding, canoeing and swimming. The behavior of one of the leaders was awful, though. He was so violent that he once broke a broomstick on the back end of one of the participants. After three weeks Harky's parents came for a visit. They discovered bruises on his back and rear end. They immediately took him home.

Harky has very positive memories of his time with the Scouts. At the age of nine he became a Cub Scout. Scouting was very important for him: 'I loved it'. Harky proudly tells that he quickly learned the required seventy skills. Since he had started scouting so young, in 1950, at age twelve, Harky became the youngest scout up to that time to earn the rank of Eagle Scout (the highest level) in the United States. Staying in a scout hut in the mountains where they had to wash in ice-cold water did him good. It was a great experience that a sickly, protected little boy could quite easily take it all on. Later Harky became a Scout Master.

Eagle Scout Award, 1950

Teenage years

Harky enjoyed his high school years much more than primary school. He had much more freedom, although this freedom was not without restrictions. Harky recalls, "The first half hour of school was spent in the so-called 'homeroom'. Two people alternately held watch: one was a dictator and when he left the room the class exploded. The other was an old, gray-haired, mild lady. When she left the room everyone remained quiet." The difference made quite an impression on Harky and taught him that nonviolence can easily go hand in hand with authority.

Harky favored team sports. He played American football because, as he mockingly states, one didn't need real coordination skills. He speaks with great respect about the trainer who taught the boys that the team was the important aspect, not the individual player. The trainer was against violence and injustice, and against smoking and drinking. Together with his mother, they organized alternative parties without alcohol.

Harky's sister, Lynn, tells me her story of the teenage years of Harky. "He was more of a good friend to me than a brother. He warned me of 'bad' boys, took me to the film, and if we had no dates we took trips in the region and had endless conversations on all kinds of subjects." Fortunately there was his faithful friend, John Innes, who visited Harky every day, whether he was in the hospital or at home.

When Harky was about thirteen or fourteen, he went to confirmation and joined the Congregational Church as did many of his peers. It was the village church he regularly attended on Sundays. The youth work was very important. Even Catholic and Jewish young people came. There always were good leaders because they had theology students from the Union Theological School in New York who did internships there.

Political climate

Harky's years in high school were during the Cold War period and the smear campaign against anything that reeked of communism. The relationship between the capitalistic West and the communistic East was very tense. Harky remembers practicing in school for the event of a nuclear attack. If the siren went off, everyone had to come inside and crawl under his desk like a turtle, as if that would protect them in any way.

When Harky was about fourteen, he bought a communist paper in New York: the *Daily Worker*. In it he read articles about the police actions against the discriminated black people in the South: news one wouldn't find in regular papers.

The execution of the (Jewish) Rosenbergs in 1953 made a deep impression on him. Harky was against the death penalty anyway, but apart from that he doubted whether they had really been guilty of spying for the Russians.

Anything that could be remotely associated with communism was suspicious. The police paid no attention to a fatal shooting that happened in a Nature Friends house close to where Harky was staying with his scouts. Someone who was booked as a communist was found dead there. They called it suicide, thinking that every living communist was one too many.

High school dropout

During his high school years, Harky once again had trouble with his health. He caught whooping cough for a second time. For some time he thought that he had cancer because the doctors could not find the cause of another illness. Eventually they discovered that a pinched nerve in his spinal column was affecting his urinary tube. Luckily it all turned out okay later. Harky's sister, Lynn, says that his health problems really influenced his years as a teenager. He had to go through several hospital admissions and operations, but it also meant music: playing guitar on the wards. A black man who could hardly read or write and whose job was sweeping the hospital floors taught Harky an important lesson: how to combine a melody and chords on the guitar. He learned something else: you can learn something from everyone. Harky's motto was, "If tomorrow is sad, at least I've had today."

Because of his hospitalizations, Harky had missed a lot of school that year. The following year he was tutored at home. When he finally could return to school, Harky was two years older than the rest of the students. The difference was too great. His condition was still not optimal, so he still missed many lessons. Finally he decided to quit school. His parents resigned to the fact that he would not become a doctor. He chose instead to become a professional musician. "I had discovered that I could make people happy with my music."

Harky as Glen Arthur

Music

Music is very important in Harky's life. His whole family had a good aptitude for music. His grandfather, Lewis William Burton, had a good voice. Before he was married he performed in minstrel shows in which white artists painted their faces black and performed a combination of famous folk music and cabaret.

When Harky was about six he took piano lessons. His teacher was called 'black', but in summer Harky's arms were darker than hers. So she was black and he was white? Harky, who had few prejudices about white and black decided that the color of skin did not matter.

A few years later Harky learned to play the violin. When he was about eleven, he found the guitar more interesting. His parents refused to pay for guitar lessons for this fickle young man, so he learned his first chords from a friend. Later his parents paid for good guitar lessons. Mr. Carlo de Filippo taught him classical guitar, and Harky had talent. Recordings of his playing were brought out on record. Every Sunday evening were the rehearsals for the Guitar and Mandolin Orchestra of his teacher. This meant he could not participate in the youth activities of the church anymore. That was too bad, but first things come first.

Under the stage name of "Glenn Arthur," Harky was successful with his virtuoso guitar playing, and he performed with his band: The Electrons. He made their own amplifiers and records.

Harky started to give guitar lessons. He enjoyed the contacts with the young people who could also come to him with their questions on matters of life. "When I was seventeen I got a job in New York. I tested guitars and designed amplifiers. I also met my idols, Chet Atkins and Les Paul! I still lived at home and could save my earnings. After a while I was laid off, however, because they said the work I was doing was superfluous."

Girlfriend

When he was seventeen, Harky got his drivers' license, a job, and a girl friend Helen. He met her through a member of the band. They were a couple for about three years and did many things together. Her personality attracted Harky. Helen was active in the youth organization of the Free Masons, and Harky joined her in various gatherings. They also went to drive-in movies in the car. Harky could get along well with her parents and was often a guest in their vacation home. Harky and Helen then went swimming or they sailed on something that was a cross between a surfboard and a sailboat on the lake.

She went to university before Harky did, far away in Pennsylvania. This meant a new start in her life, and she returned his ring. Harky understood, and his heart was not broken. There was enough in his life to make it worthwhile!

—2—

Never Expected and Yet Fulfilled

For a high school dropout, it didn't look like an academic career would be possible for Harky. But his life has taken unexpected turns.

Touched by the spirit

In 1957 the famous evangelist, Billy Graham, held a religious revival in New York City. Harky relates, "My girl friend and I attended. I was certainly not an uncritical admirer of Billy Graham, and I had my doubts about his approach, but I still remember his sermon on King Manasseh and the hymn that was sung then:

> Just as I am, without one plea,
> And that thy blood was shed for me,
> And that thou bidst me come to thee,
> O Lamb of God, I come, I come.

In spite of myself, I stood up when Billy Graham called those who wanted to dedicate their lives to Jesus to come forward. I felt as though I had been pulled out of my chair, and I regarded it as something supernatural. I still do. I am absolutely not sensitive to suggestion, so this cannot be explained psychologically. I went forward with the intention of devoting the rest of my life to His service." Through this experience and through his experience with the young people to whom Harky gave guitar lessons, Harky began to play with the idea of becoming a minister.

Harky began studying the differences and similarities in approaches to religion in various denominations.

Harky, "I read many books and visited many churches. I felt at home with many, but especially with the Quakers. The Quakers are pacifists, are against the death penalty, reject slavery, and have done much for the acceptance of the mentally disordered and for the rights of Native Americans. I still have one foot in the Quaker world. I was not really taught pacifism at home. That I have become a peacemaker is thanks to the Quakers. And of course, to Martin Luther King, but that came later." During one of the meetings of the Quakers, Harky was told by an unknown person that he should go beyond the Quaker community. He considered this to be another encouragement to become a minister.

Harky recalls, "I had a prophetic dream at that time which consisted of three parts. I first dreamd of a Dutch Reformed Church which I had never visited before. Then I was in a church without walls. And in the last dream I was in a strange building. I went outside and saw the stars falling and the earth open up. Two of the prophecies were fulfilled. Two years later I worked in a Dutch Reformed Church. I recognize the church without walls in the worldwide peace movement of which I am a part.

The third?"

Bloomfield College

To become a minister seemed impossible. At the time that Harky quit school, a student was not allowed to attend university without a high school diploma. Fortunately, this changed soon after and Harky could do an entrance test. In the fall of 1959, he was admitted to *Bloomfield College*, a small Presbyterian educational institution in Bloomfield, New Jersey, close to home. Most of the four hundred students either lived at home or with family and traveled back and forth. A few lived in the dormitory on the campus. Harky, who was 21 by then, remained living at home.

Harky, "During my first study year, I saw a small advertisement from a Dutch Reformed Church, in Ridgefield Park, New Jersey, a village three quarters of an hour away. They were looking for someone. I thought they wanted someone to do practical work, like exchanging storm windows for screens. (During the winter, storm windows had to be placed before the windows because of the cold weather. In spring the storms were exchanged for screens.) In the course of the interview, it turned they needed a youth leader. I got the job. The first prophecy was fulfilled.

The minister there was a very unusual man. He prided himself that he never used notes and stood next to the pulpit. Fortunately the service never lasted longer than an hour. One Saturday evening about nine o'clock I received a phone call, asking if I could lead the service the next morning. I had very good time with that congregation."

Bloomfield College was known for its outstanding professors, and Harky was especially enthusiastic about his professor of philosophy. "I had chosen history as a major and took philosophy only because it was mandatory. To my surprise, I loved the subject and, thanks to the inspiring professor, received all high marks. I also had two professors of religion with differing theologies. One was liberal. He was honest enough to admit that he let the papers of his students fall down the stairs and gave them the mark according to where they landed. But he was very intelligent, and I learned much from him. The other was older and much more conservative. I owe most of my thanks to him because, after my first year, he advised me to work in a church consisting of mostly elderly people. I wasn't enthusiastic; I liked working with young people."

Undenominational Church, Denville, New Jersey, 1960

"When I had to choose what I would do in my second year, I had a dream which helped me make my choice. I walked through the streets and came to an open space. There were elderly people there who needed help. I heard them more than I saw them. It was clear to me: I should do what my conservative professor had advised me, work for a church with only elderly people. For over one year I preached every Sunday in the Undenominational Church in Denville, New Jersey. What I did there was part of the reason that I was chosen to do a Junior Year Abroad."

Junior Year Abroad

In his third year, 1961-1962, Harky studied philosophy and theology at the *University of London*, England, after completing a summer course in Edinburgh, Scotland. In London he became acquainted with class discrimination. You couldn't just go sit anywhere in a pub. He found it awful that there was a separate part for workers and one for the rich.

In London he also encountered the *Ban the Bomb* action groups, which were at their peak during this period of the Cold War. A classmate took him along to his first demonstration. He never lost the demonstration virus he caught that day. A conversation with a pacifist classmate one night was a turning point for his theology. "OK" I said to him, "for myself I would not kill, but how can I protect my sister?" He said, 'How can you think that God loves your sister more than the sister of someone who lives in Moscow?' I had no answer to this question."

The rebuilt *Coventry Cathedral*, Coventry, England, made a deep impression on Harky during his travels through England. The Germans had bombed this important cathedral, and only the outside walls remained standing. Coventry's inhabitants refused to be dragged into the spiral of revenge and violence and began the Coventry prayer. This prayer for peace and reconciliation is prayed around the world, also in the Netherlands, every Friday at 12:30pm. Harky still regularly uses the words of the prayer in his services. After the war the cathedral was quickly rebuilt, but the damaged church still stands as a symbol of war and peace. Harky was moved to see the cross made of the charred wood and nails that had remained.

Harky wrote a paper about church architecture and the role it can play for peace and reconciliation.

Coventry Cross, Coventry, England

The Coventry Litany of Reconciliation

FATHER FORGIVE

All have sinned
and fallen short of the glory of God.

The HATRED which divides nation from nation, race from race, class from class,
Father forgive

The COVETOUS desires of people and nations to possess what is not their own,
Father forgive

The GREED which exploits the work of human hands and lays waste the earth,
Father forgive

Our ENVY of the welfare and happiness of others,
Father forgive

Our INDIFFERENCE to the plight of the imprisoned, the homeless, the refugee,
Father forgive

The LUST which dishonours the bodies of men, women and children,
Father forgive

The PRIDE which leads us to trust in ourselves and not in God,
Father forgive

Be kind to one another, tenderhearted,
forgiving one another,
as God in Christ forgave you.

In 1962 Harky made a trip from London to the Middle East during Easter vacation. It was a special arrangement for two weeks. He visited Israel and several neighboring countries. The trip made a deep impression on Harky–to walk on the ground where Jesus walked. He has kept a card with dried flowers from the Holy Land all these years. In Egypt Harky saw what hunger can do to people. He saw a man step on a little girl's hand until she let go of the coins she had received. Apparently this is what hunger can make a person do.

Never Expected and Yet Fulfilled

Lynn, 1960

Traveling through Europe

In the summer of 1962, Harky's sister, Lynn, came to Europe—a gift from her parents for getting her high school diploma. She and Harky received money to make a trip through Europe and to buy a car, which would be shipped to America as a second-hand car. The money should have lasted about two to three weeks if they had stayed in hotels on the way. Harky figured out that they could travel much longer if they camped out. They bought a Volkswagen car in which they could also sleep. First they went to England, Scotland and Wales, and then took the boat to France. Because of their camping, the trip was so inexpensive it lasted two and a half months! That meant that they could afford fresh fruit and vegetables and sometimes entrance to a swimming pool, midget golf or local sound and light show. Partly because of the meeting of so many fellow campers, it was an immensely educational trip in which they traveled through many West

European countries. According to Lynn, the journey widened their outlook on customs, religions, family values and political systems.

In 1963 Harky graduated. He acquired his BA in philosophy, cum laud.

Memories of Bloomfield College

The 1963 yearbook of Bloomfield College contains pictures of students and staff. Striking is that only a few colored students and a rare black staff member are seen. On seeing a picture of his sister Lynn, he recalls that she, just as his mother, had contributed significantly to this book. Lynn took the pictures for the year book and developed them in her darkroom. His mother provided the accompanying texts.

There are several handwritten notes of Harky's fellow classmates who express their thanks to Harky's mother. Apparently this was his mother's book. On one page, Barbara, Harky's girlfriend at that time, wrote, "I know that Lynn and Harky are showing the strength and character which you and Mr. Klinefelter have transmitted to them." Also, Harky's best friend, Louis Mueller wrote, "My acquaintance with you and your wonderful family has been and still is a high spot and joy to me."

More memories arise:

"I was on the soccer team. Soccer was a cheap sport. You didn't need an expensive protective clothing like in football. It also had a much lower status. Our star of the team was a Hungarian student who played in his socks."

Harky recalls, "In Bloomfield College my best friend was Lou Mueller. He had been a soldier in Germany and there he learned to ride a motorcycle. He came to the college on his motorcycle every day. That was something quite extraordinary. Lou was an agnostic, and we often talked about philosophy and discussed the questions of life. At my graduation I received a framed copy of Dürer's painting, *Praying Hands,* from him."

Although Harky lived at home, he sometimes spent the night at the dormitory on the campus. One of the students told the school authority if fellow classmates misbehaved. When this tattletale came back after Christmas holidays, his room was filled with 23 Christmas trees (a nonviolent action).

Harky wrote a blues number about life in the dormitory.

Bloomfield College, Bloomfield, New Jersey, 1959-1963

When Harky started at Bloomfield in 1959, America was in the middle of the Cuba crisis. He remembers the Free Speech Movement at the *University of California* at Berkeley, the first student protest movement in the US. The protesting students were regarded as being communists. In the US, especially at the height of the Cold War, this often resulted in a harsh jail sentence. Harky remembers that the president of Bloomfield College was on the side of the students. During a meeting of the Free Speech Movement, he read a letter from his brother who had been a minister in Germany and had written in 1938, "Thank God for Adolph Hitler–he is saving us from the Communists." This letter made a deep impression on Harky. At that moment he realized that most ministers in Germany supported Hitler because they were afraid of communists, and that in America the same thing was going on. Communists were demonized. Harky would have liked to ask the German pro-Hitler ministers how they came to this belief and if they had really believed Hitler was a good ruler.

Becoming a minister

Harky's father thought it wonderful that his son wanted to study theology. Two days before his death, he and Harky visited several universities. Harky had received grants for three universities. Fortunately, Harky's father preferred *Yale University* in New Haven, Connecticut. It was so far away that Harky could not remain living at home, and this is exactly what he wanted: to stand on his own two feet. The socially progressive atmosphere appealed to him too.

Harky was twenty-five when his father unexpectedly passed away, a month before Harky's graduation at Bloomfield College. Klinefelter Sr. was in the hospital for X-rays and suddenly died of heart failure. This strong man who had toted coal as a student and who had amazed Harky by holding the car up while his wife changed the tire, was no longer with them. The last words Harky heard from him were, "I wish you good luck in the seminary."

Harky and son Douwe at Yale University, New Haven, Connecticut, 2008

In 1963 Harky began his theology studies at the Yale University's theological seminary, *Yale Divinity School*, in New Haven, Connecticut. Part of the course consisted of internships involving helping ministers with youth work. During his first year, he interned in New Britain, Connecticut. Many inhabitants were of the working class, and he learned much about the life of the common man. The congregation was warm and creative. The minister was an intelligent man with a passion for poetry.

In his second year at Yale, Harky was involved with the youth group of a local church in New Haven. With them, he visited the black church of Homer McCall whom he knew from the dormitory. The teenagers loved it: much more lively than their own boring white church. Homer also studied theology and he and Harky became friends. Their friendship still exists!

Homer's home church was Ebenezer Baptist Church in Atlanta, Georgia. This was the church of Martin Luther King, Sr. His son, Dr. Martin Luther King, Jr., was the assistant minister. Through Homer and Ebenezer, Harky became involved in the Civil Rights Movement and later on with the organization of Martin Luther King, the SCLC (The Southern Christian Leadership Conference). From his teens on, Harky admired Dr. King and followed him on TV. The involvement with the civil rights movement took on such proportions that Harky went to work as intern for two years with the SCLC and moved to Atlanta, Georgia.

Annelies, Atlanta, Georgia, 1965

The Life of Peace Apostle Harcourt Klinefelter

Meeting a Dutch girl in Atlanta, Georgia

And there she came from overseas, the love of Harky's life. Annelies Koopmans came to Atlanta in 1965 as part of an exchange program organized by the Dutch Mennonites. In the summer of 1965, Harky and other staff members lived in Dr. King's old house. The backyard was adjacent to that of the Mennonite House. In this house Mennonite exchange visitors from different countries lived. Bert Alberda, Harky's best friend who had come a year earlier, also lived there. He also worked in the office of the SCLC.

Bert told Harky of a Dutch girl who had just arrived and who would be celebrating her 20th birthday the next week. Together they organized a party for her. The spark between Harky and Annelies ignited quite quickly. Harky took Annelies out for pizza by candlelight, a drive-in movie and a picnic in Stone Mountain Park. Harky heard awful guttural sounds on his short wave radio and Annelies said, "Oh that is Dutch."

Annelies has vivid memories of that time. She tells that Harky always wanted to know what was going on in the world. She remembers him running back and forth between different TV's to see how the different networks presented the latest news.

During Annelies's year in America, she visited Harky's parents' house several times so his mother Lucille knew her well. Lucille hoped that Harky and Annelies would get married before Annelies returned to the Netherlands. But according to Annelies, that was impossible: marrying someone your parents had never met. The night before Annelies left, she telephoned her minister in her home town of Drachten. He put the couple at ease saying, "If it's God's will, it will work out." Annelies took the boat back to the Netherlands in the summer of 1966. Harky put her on the boat, but was so distraught; he wanted to swim after her.

Annelies had a visa for one year. After that she had to leave the US for at least two years. This rule was followed very strictly. A friend lawyer helped them. They applied for an exception to this law on the basis of an exceptional hardship ruling. But, you had to be married first, in order to apply for this exception.

While she was away, Harky wrote letters to Annelies. He also learned Dutch from a book which caused him to learn the wrong pronunciation. His pronunciation has never really improved.

When Harky took the train to Drachten to be married, a Belgian passenger taught Harky what he should say upon meeting Annelies' father. *Blij je te ontmoeten.* ["Pleased to meet you."] This made a good impression.

Harky and Annelies got married on December 29, 1966, in Drachten, the Netherlands, Annelies' hometown. The service was held in three languages: Dutch, English and Frisian, the mother language of Annelies. The next day the couple went to Amsterdam to the American Embassy to apply for the exceptional hardship ruling.

During their honeymoon in the Netherlands, Harky felt the same way he felt as a child. During their visits to Annelies' friends, he heard all the conversations going on around him, but could not understand much of it. He was astonished to see the mourners at Annelies' grandfather's funeral (January 9, 1967) walk with the casket three times around the graveyard.

In February 1967 Annelies and Harky flew back to the U.S. with the required papers. They spent the first two months living with Harky's mother. During this time, Harky worked with Bill Stein, the PR man who had worked for the SCLC as a volunteer, on a documentary of the Selma March, the peaceful demonstration against racism of 1965. Upon moving back to Atlanta, their first 'home' was a tent in the camp ground at Stone Mountain Park where they had picnicked during their courtship. "That was a wonderful summer. We went swimming in the lake every evening."

Living for "free"

After a while they lived for free with someone who was involved with the training work of the SCLC. As compensation, Harky had to take the hostess to the airport whenever she had to travel, which was often. "It was terrible. She was never ready at the time appointed, so I had to drive dangerously fast to be able to make the flight, often during rush hour. Usually we were at the airport in the nick of time. The ninth time she actually missed her flight. Later I realized why she wanted to be there as late as possible. She was afraid of flying, so if she were there at the last minute, she had something else to worry about. But it still bothers me. I am still always afraid I will miss the plane when I have to travel . . . Stress, stress, stress."

Harky and Annelies finally found a flat for themselves and lived in Atlanta until Harky decided to go back to Yale to finish his theological studies. This was upon recommendation of Dr. Martin Luther King, Jr.

How did this important contact come about? Read the next chapter.

—3—

At the Side of Dr. Martin Luther King, Jr.

DISCRIMINATION AGAINST THE BLACK population? Harky had never paid much attention to it. In the second year of his theological studies he was taken by Homer McCall to a meeting where Dr. King was to speak. "It was my first Civil Rights Rally. The room was overcrowded but we found a place in the wings. When Dr. King and his police escort entered the stage, he recognized my friend. He walked past all the dignitaries to greet him, 'How are your studies going, Homer?' I found this amazing."

Selma and the voting rights campaign

In the spring of 1965, Martin Luther King began a campaign for voting rights in the South. On March 7, 1965, a day which has gone down in history as "Bloody Sunday," defenseless demonstrators in Selma, Alabama were brutally beaten up. Seventy people were severely injured.

Reverend James Reeb, a white minister from Boston, came to Selma to protest. He was recognized as a "nigger lover" and was beaten with baseball bats by several whites. Two days later he died of his injuries. During a memorial service organized by Yale University, the words of a minister who had just returned from Selma deeply impressed Harky, "There has been a crucifixion in Selma; we need people for a social resurrection." Harky needed no more than one night to decide; the next day he drove more than 1300 kilometers to Selma.

"The Berlin Wall" (police barricade), Selma, Alabama, 1965

When Harky arrived in Selma, he immediately went to the *Berlin Wall*. "This was the name given to the police barricade where demonstrators and police stood facing each other. On one side stood the scared police officers, on the other side a handful of people who had gathered to pray and to witness. There was a group of children singing: '*I love everybody, I love Dr. King, I love Reverend Abernathy.*' But they also sang: '*I love state troopers, I love George Wallace.*' And that while the state police and Governor Wallace were responsible for the violence their fathers and mothers had experienced shortly before!" That was Harky's first experience of the nonviolent character of the demonstrations.

Harky brought with him the portable Philips tape recorder which he had brought back from Europe. He wanted to make recordings in order to report his experiences in the journal of the Yale Divinity School, *Reflections*. Such a device was a rarity in those days.

Harky's interest in recording techniques came from his father. During the war, his mother, Lucille Klinefelter gave her husband a disc recorder as a Christmas gift. That was the newest thing going. With this recorder, his father made recordings of the festivities when the war was over as well as Harky's guitar playing. Tape recorders for home use came on the market only in the fifties.

With his knowledge of recording, Harky would soon become indispensable for the Southern Christian Leadership Conference (SCLC), the organization of Martin Luther King.

Even before the famous Selma March, Harky and Bill Stein, a PR professional who also worked as a volunteer in the movement, were responsible for contacts with the press. Recordings of important speeches and interviews were sent to the media by telephone. Through the efforts of Harky and Bill, news was spread that certainly would not have otherwise have been picked up by the media.

In Montgomery, Alabama, the final terminus of the march, Harky recorded Martin Luther King's speech. He and Bill Stein then set up a temporary news office. They spread the news that Viola Liuzzo was shot to death after the march as she drove marchers back home to Selma. They stopped using the office when they received word from the FBI that the Ku Klux Klan was preparing an attack on their improvised news agency. In retrospect, the question arises if the FBI actually had this information or if they used this threat as a ploy to end Harky's and Bill's news reports.

Later on Harky interviewed people who had walked the whole march and he and Bill made a radio program called *Sounds from Selma*.

The most impressive narrative was that of a girl aged about nineteen or twenty. She told of her experiences in inspiring words. She was so brave; despite her blisters she continued the whole way. She said, "*They only hurt when I stop . . . "I'm not afraid. I mean, one day I must die. I would rather die for something good than for nothing. I think this is a good reason for dying."*

If Harky had not brought the tape recorder along, the world would have missed many speeches and sermons of Dr. King, and also many news items concerning the Civil Rights Movement. Harky would probably also not have gotten to know this charismatic leader so personally. He considers the course of events not as coincidence but as providence.

After the Easter vacation Harky returned to Yale. During the summer vacation, he went back to SCLC as a volunteer to help, among other things, with the *Summer Community Organizing and Political Education Program* (SCOPE) to register voters.

That summer there was a demonstration in Albany, Georgia. Harky went there to make recordings of the event. On the way back, he and his black colleague ran out of gas in Ku Klux Klan-territory.

Harky, "The animosity towards black people in that area was enormous. We really were in mortal danger. My colleague hid in the bushes while I tried hitchhiking and luckily received a ride. At the closest gas station, since I had no jerry can, I received a watering can full of gas (very dangerous!). But, in the end, I was not allowed to take the gas with me. A farmer drove to the gas station, jumped out of his car, and told the owner that there had also been a black man in my car. I was afraid the owner would throw a burning cigarette into the can. While continuing to the next station, I began to wonder what kind of a person my driver was. If he belonged to the Ku Klux Klan, I was very much in danger. At the next station they refused to serve us; someone had called to warn them. Finally, at the third gas station I was able to buy gas. When we got back to the car, the driver who had given me the ride wanted no money for his gas although he had driven quite a distance." He said, 'I want you to know that not all the people in this area think like the people we met at the gas stations." What Harky especially remembers about this incident is the confrontation with his fear and own prejudice. "Through this event, I have never forgotten the message that not all inhabitants of Georgia are racists."

At that time there was talk of a possible prohibition of the Ku Klux Klan. Dr. King was very much opposed to this. He argued, "You have to grant your enemies the same freedom you wish for yourself."

SCLC office, Atlanta, Georgia

Assistant Director of Public Relations–1965–1969

At the end of the summer, Harky officially became a member of the SCLC staff. He was allowed to use his job as an internship for his studies. Harky was not the only white person on the staff. There was the Director of the Public Relation Department, Thom Offenburger, and one of the Directors of the Dialog Program, Rachel Du Bois. Other ethnicities were also represented. A Chinese-American woman, Mu Sing Lee, was another Dialog Program Director. So we had black, white and yellow on the staff.

In SCLC Harky discovered a spiritual authenticity which appealed to him more than the intellectual approach which was common at the university. There it was everyone out for him/herself.

The trust that Dr. King placed in Harky impressed him very much. At a certain point that summer, Harky came to be suspected. He was sitting in some kind of closet to find a quiet place to work on his recording and that looked suspicious. Was he maybe a spy for the FBI? Dr. King was consulted, and he backed Harky up. Luckily so, because Harky asked himself if he even wanted to continue living if SCLC should throw him out.

Singer Joan Baez sings during the SCLC staff retreat. Second person to her right is Harky, next to Dr. Martin Luther King Jr. at Frogmore, South Carolina, 1966

Dr. Martin Luther King Speaks on the radio

Harky was responsible for taping the speeches and sermons of Dr. King. Dr. King required an audience to preach passionately. Once he held a sermon in a studio but that was incredibly boring. That was the reason that Dr. King initially did not favor radio broadcasts.

Harky and Bill Stein edited a sermon as an example of what could be broadcast on a 29-minute radio program. They went to see Dr. King to get permission to make more of such recordings. King was preparing to address a gathering of 250,000 people in front of the UN in the afternoon and to give another speech at the Riverside Church in New York City in the evening. Dr. King took time out to talk to Harky and Bill. He agreed that their condensing his sermons for radio programing was a good idea.

That day in NYC was exactly one year before King's death. He spoke against the war in Vietnam, earning him heavy criticism. He was called a traitor. Dr. King emphasized that he did not protest in anger, but out of disappointment in his homeland. He said, "There can be no great disappointment without great love." People asked him to limit his concern to racial segregation, but he said, "Injustice anywhere is a threat to justice everywhere."

Reverend King

Eventually, Harky edited many recordings of sermons for the weekly radio program named *Dr. Martin Luther King Speaks*. Programs were sent out over many years to over 300 radio stations; some stations still air this programming today. Shortening the sermons to twenty-nine minutes each was a task which took days.

Dr. King was always concerned for other people. He realized that Harky had taken on a large job, so he phoned Harky to tell him how he made his sermons. Dr. King had listened to the first edited sample and approved that they should continue, but he felt that it would be handy for Harky to know something about his principles and how he structured his sermons. Harky has always remembered what Dr. King said:

- You should only say things that you believe in
- An essay is to inform, a sermon is to convince
- An appeal must be made to the intellect, the emotions, and the will

- A sermon has a number of fixed elements
- A tantalizing proposition/theory
- Three points, with each point containing three examples:
  - one for the intellectual
  - a second one for the average churchgoer
  - a third one for the illiterate (examples were often humorous and from his own life)
- A summary
- An ending (often with quotes which he had used in previous speeches)

According to Harky, Dr. King was a superb preacher. This was a result of his being the son and grandson of black ministers with their traditional use of repetition. Dr. King was also highly educated. He had studied an extra four years in *Boston University* for a PhD, and he learned a lot from Shakespeare who wrote his plays both in intricate poetry to appeal to the intellectuals and in bawdy humor to appeal to the uneducated.

Dr. King usually wrote his sermons down. Harky recalls that, if King put his foot on the amplifier, that was under the pulpit, Harky knew he was going to improvise. The phrase *"I have a dream"* from his famous speech in Washington in 1963 was something he had picked up from a teenage girl in Georgia. Just before his speech in Washington, Mahalia Jackson encouraged King to use the phrase. She said, *"Tell them about the dream."* What followed was off the cuff—and unforgettable.

Chicago

During the winter of 1966, Dr. King went to Chicago. This journey was a turning point in the movement; now the northern states also became his work area. This demanded a different approach. In the South there was an easy, clearly visible enemy; in the North, the situation was more complicated. There, for example, real estate cartels earned huge sums of money with *"blockbusting."* Dr. King wanted to call attention to this practice. In blockbusting, real estate agents surreptitiously got home owners in white neighborhoods to sell their houses because of fear of devaluation should black people come to live in the neighborhood. Once the houses were available, they were sold for exorbitant prices to black people searching for an escape from the overcrowded ghettos.

March Against Fear 1966

James Meredith, the first black student at the *University of Mississippi*, wanted to organize a march from Memphis to Jackson, the capital of Mississippi, in order to encourage the black population to register to vote. He was shot down but survived. Although SCLC did not want to fight a war on two fronts, the North and the South, they decided that this was the moment in which they could no longer remain on the sidelines.

During this march in Mississippi, Dr. King was to speak at different places along the way. Harky set up loudspeakers outside the churches where the crowds flocked to listen. He himself rode the march with his recording equipment in a car—of all things, a Cadillac! Harky cherishes the picture that was taken during the March of himself and Dr. King.

Dr. King and Harky, March Against Fear, Missisippi, 1966

At the Side of Dr. Martin Luther King, Jr.

Harky tells the story behind the photo taken by Bob Fitch on June 24, 1966

"As Assistant Director for Public Relations for SCLC, I accompanied Dr. King during the March Against Fear in 1966. During this march, from Memphis, Tennessee, to Jackson, Mississippi, we were constantly exposed to danger. The most dangerous moment was entering Philadelphia, Mississippi, where two years earlier three civil rights activists—Schwerner, Chaney and Goodman—had been kidnapped and murdered. In the lion's den, we wanted to hold a prayer service in their memory. As we approached the town square, I saw angry people everywhere. We were outnumbered. To my surprise the crowd was quiet during the speech of Dr. King. When Rev. Ralph Abernathy (Dr. King's right-hand man) began his prayer, the silence was over. The crowd began shouting. While the marchers repeated the words 'Father, forgive them, for they know not what they do,' the horror began. A crowd of several hundred people, with all kinds of weapons ranging from guns to homemade clubs, shouted death threats against the marchers. Above the shouting we could hear loud noises. Were they shots or powerful fireworks? We were afraid that the fireworks were being used to mask the sound of gunfire. The first "cherry bomb" hit a girl and injured her leg.

The marchers sought a safe haven from firecrackers that were coming down left and right of us. Then I saw a black man lying on the road. It looked like he was having an epileptic seizure. I went to him, and a white nurse joined me. We were surrounded. The other marchers could then escape because the attention of the masses that was now focused on us. All around us were hostile people, and there was no visible ally, not even the press. We feared for our lives and saw no way out. The furious screams kept sounding louder! 'Let that nigger die, don't you see that he is a slave? Grab them! Kill them!' It was hopeless. Only a miracle could save us. Andrew Young, vice president of SCLC, was one of the last demonstrators to leave. He said to Harky 'Goodbye,' and not 'until next time.' He thought Harky's days were numbered."

"Then I looked up and saw a pickup truck with two black policemen coming through the crowd toward us. They were specially hired for the day to help the city improve its image. Just like Moses who went through the Red Sea, the crowd parted. We lifted the unconscious man into the truck and jumped in after him."

"While we were trying to crouch down as low as was possible, a firecracker was thrown into the truck. The cherry bomb landed just in front of the face of the unconscious man. It was about to explode. I thought, "It's his eyes or my hand." Then I thought better and stepped on the fireworks. The firecracker exploded, but the explosion for the most part was converted into heat under my shoe. The only result was a very hot foot. The sole of my shoe rescued the eyes of our soul brother. We drove on and finally reached the rest of the marchers. Now we heard the cheerful sounds of freedom songs rising up to God instead of furious cries."

"Looking back, I realize that the words, 'Father, forgive them,' and our action as "Good Samaritans" had appealed to the conscience of the crowd and their humanity prevailed. That is the essence of nonviolence as Dr. King preached."

"Was it providence that I am able to tell the tale? I do not know. But I do know that I would do it again, because even if we had been killed, we would have ensured that Martin Luther King and the rest of the marchers could escape."

During the same march, the term '*Black Power*' appeared in the media for the first time. It referred to the non-pacifistic faction of black protests. Dr. King's response was classic. He asked, "Who were the people who had a history of murdering individuals and throwing their bodies into the river? And now people request of me that I should sink to that level! No. Never." And he added that there were white people who had died for the freedom of the blacks, adding, among others, the name of Reverend James Reeb.

The nonviolence of Dr. King was characterized by love, an unconditional following of a radical commandment. Not only he, but nearly everyone around him, radiated respect and forgiveness. A slogan of the civil rights movement was, "to save black men's bodies and white men's souls." Only love can break the vicious circle of fear and violence. Furthermore, Dr. King said, "We have a power that is greater than the atomic bomb. An atomic bomb can only destroy. Love has the power to change people's attitudes. Love is the only power that can change an enemy into a friend."

During the march, which took nearly three weeks, the participants slept in large circus tents. In Canton the police ordered the camp to be cleared. They fired in two types of gas: tear gas and the heavier nausea gas. One circus tent collapsed. Dr. King had to leave the stage (improvised on a truck) but Harky was still on the truck. He inhaled the gas and thought he was going to die. Sometime later he accompanied a wounded woman to the hospital. Annelies, Harky's sweetheart saw pictures of this encounter on TV and immediately left for Jackson. Harky says, "Every time I went on a march, I didn't know if I would come back." Although taking part in nonviolent protests was absolutely not without risks, Harky even went to a gathering of the Ku Klux Klan as a part of a group consisting of black and white protesters. The team spirit and enthusiasm of the movement caused him not to be afraid.

Related activities

Another part of Harky's responsibility, together with Bert Alberda, was that of answering the letters Dr. King received. King was averse of any signs of hero worship, so any requests that reeked of this, such as the request of artists to be allowed to paint their idol, were quickly denied.

Although he did not like it, Martin Luther King accepted the fact that he was seen as the personification of the Civil Rights Movement. If Harky told a radio station that the SCLC was planning to set up an encampment close the government buildings, they were not interested. If he said that Dr. King said that the sun rose in the east and went down in the west, they gladly would broadcast it. It would be foolish not to use the reputation of Martin Luther King!

Harky regrets that the person of Martin Luther King became so famous, while his method of nonviolent social change is so little talked about. Exactly the opposite is what he himself would have wanted.

Besides his work as media director, Harky gave dialog trainings aimed at mutual understanding between whites and blacks. The Directors of the SCLC's Dialog Program, Rachel Dubois, an elderly Quaker woman, and Mu Sung Li, the woman with whom Harky and Annelies had stayed temporarily, were pioneers in this area. According to them, the key to reconciliation between blacks and whites was to go back to ones' childhood. A child has no prejudices. Talking about former memories is a very good way of closing the gap. It often appears that people, to their own astonishment, share certain memories. A white and a black woman both appeared to know what ash cake was: a bread loaf baked in ashes without using an oven pan. Both the black and white woman had experienced poverty in their youth, and this provided a bond. Many hymns were also common to both.

In the presence of Martin Luther King, people felt lifted beyond themselves. He did not judge people by the color of their skin, but by the content of their character. He saw not what they had been, but what they were now. More importantly, he saw what they could become, and inspired people to grow.

Personal experiences with the King family

Dr. King was easy to approach. During the Selma March, Harky could simply go to him and ask what he should do with the recordings he had made. Dr. King joked that he could give them to the FBI. Harky also was impressed how democratic the staff meetings were.

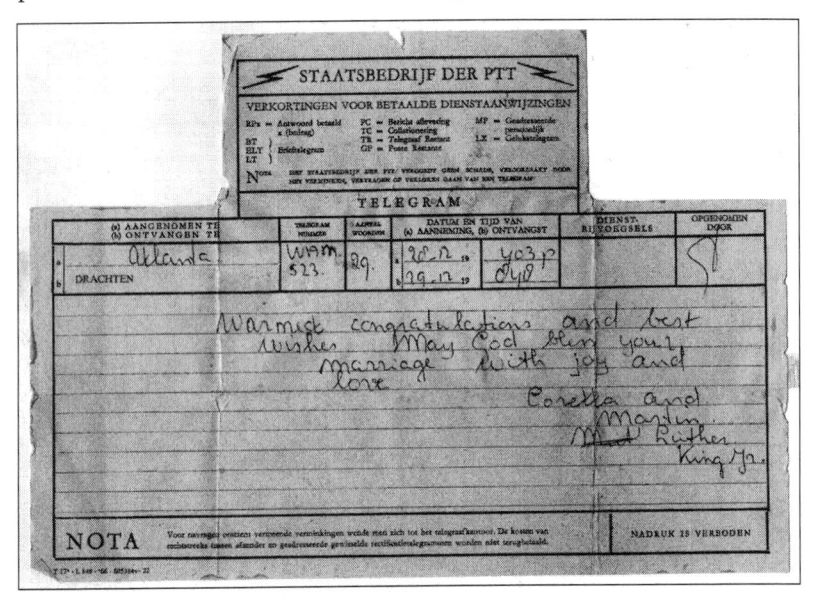

When Harky and Annelies married in December of 1966 in the Netherlands, they received a telegram from Dr. King. Harky carefully keeps the telegram and a letter of recommendation which Dr. King wrote for him when he departed for the Netherlands. It is a hearty and affectionate recommendation showing personal appreciation. The letter contains the address of the SCLC and the names of the President (Martin Luther King Jr.), the Treasurer (Ralph Abernathy) and the Executive Director (Andrew J. Young), It is dated December 5, 1966, and addressed "To whom it may concern." Harky had asked for this letter because he did not know how long he and Annelies would have to stay in the Netherlands. Fortunately, they could return after six weeks.

AT THE SIDE OF DR. MARTIN LUTHER KING, JR.

---

334 Auburn Ave., N.E.
Atlanta, Georgia 30303
Telephone 522-1420

Southern Christian Leadership Conference

Martin Luther King Jr., *President*   Ralph Abernathy, *Treasurer*   Andrew J. Young, *Executive Director*

December 5, 1966

TO WHOM IT MAY CONCERN:

Harcourt Klinefelter has been a faithful worker for the Southern Christian Leadership Conference since he left Yale Divinity School in 1965 to aid us in our struggle for human rights and justice. His assistance to me has been invaluable.

As Audio-Visual Director of our Public Relations Department, he has been instrumental in helping to bring before the world the injustices of our society. This work often exposed him to danger, but he was steadfast in his courage and his commitment to non-violence.

Mr. Klinefelter's dedication to serve humanity stems from a deep religious faith. He has donated much of his time to our church, which he attends regularly.

Harcourt is well-equipped for a variety of endeavors. He has acquired technical skills in his work with us, and has utilized his formal education by helping us develop our programs for bringing about a more equitable system. He studied at Edinburgh University and King's College, University of London, and he graduated cum laude from Bloomfield College in New Jersey with a degree in philosophy. Yale Divinity School extended his internship in order that he might continue his important work with us.

Harcourt Klinefelter is our loyal friend, and I feel certain that he is worthy of your trust and confidence.

Sincerely,

Martin Luther King, Jr.

Km

In 1967 Harky went with Martin Luther King when he and his children visited an amusement park. The children had received free tickets to the roller coaster. Father naturally had to go with them. Before the ride, Dr. King said seriously, "Harcourt there is something I have to tell you right now." Harky wondered what great words of wisdom he would tell him. Dr. King went on to say, "Harcourt, this is a very frightening ride!" He was right; it was a frightening ride. That Dr. King ventured to take a ride on a roller coaster he knew was frightening impressed Harky. Even more impressive to Harky was that the undaunted Dr. King admitted to having been afraid!

Harky, "At the request of Dr. King, I remained with the SCLC for a second year. At the end of that second year Dr. King invited Annelies and me to come to dinner. He said, 'You should go back to Yale to finish your study. Otherwise you will never do it.' That was the fall of 1967. I don't know if he said that only because he knew me so well. He knew that my work with the SCLC was more important to me than my studies. Maybe a contributing factor was that he had a premonition of his impending death. In like manner, King had just given his wife artificial flowers for the first time. Definitely, I would never have finished my study without this encouragement. At the time studying seemed so unimportant."

At home with the King family

Harky says, "One day I was asked by Mrs. King to fix the tape recorder in their home. It turned out to be an old and heavy thing that they used to record personal things. Their house was in one of the black slums. Dr. King chose to live there saying, 'I want to be reminded every day for whom I work.' Dr. King lived on his salary as assistant minister. He gave everything he earned in speaking and writing away to the Civil Rights Movement. As head of the organization, SCLC, he received one dollar a year as a symbolic salary. Like other middle class families, the King family had difficulties in making ends meet. The living room was austerely furnished. There was a small statue of Gandhi, his Nobel Peace Prize, and a large painting of a woman in front of a mirror. On one side she was white, and on the other, black. The bedroom was at the back of the house. This was for safety reasons, because a bomb had exploded on the porch of their home in Montgomery. The house was not protected by an alarm system. The children simply opened the front door if the bell rang."

"We took the tape recorder out of the bedroom and brought it in to the living room. It took a lot of time to fix the tape recorder. While I was working on it, I had a good conversation with Mrs. King. She was also closely involved in the peace movement. It got late, and Mrs. King asked, 'Will you eat dinner with us?'

I said, 'I don't want to make extra work for you.' 'No,' she said, 'that's no problem. Martin often invites unexpected guests. That's why I always have extra food in the house.' I said, 'If that is so, then I would really like to stay!'

Dr. King came in and I said, 'Dr. King, I do not feel worthy enough to sit with you at the table.' He replied, *'Now Harcourt, you make it necessary for me to preach a long sermon about how all men are equal.'"*

What better answer could you find to put someone at ease!

Back at Yale

Paul Harris was a fellow student of Harky's at Yale Divinity School in 1967-1968. Harky and Paul each worked part time in a congregation: Harky in a white church and Paul, in a black church. Harky suggested organizing combined activities for the youth in both churches. It went well and stimulated their friendship. They became friends and still are.

Paul remembers the wonderful stories that Harky told and the smile that would fly across his face. The stories were colored by his subtle humor and his passion for justice. He also had to think of the day that Martin Luther King was assassinated. Harky came with the news which shocked the entire community of theology students. It was decided that Harky would represent the Yale fellowship at the funeral.

Paul, "Harky's recordings of the speeches of Dr. King are important for everyone who is committed to peace and justice. The passion with which both Harky and Annelies work toward a peaceful and just society continues to resonate in everyone who knows them."

Paul and his wife Sally enjoy the warm friendship with Harky and Annelies and are deeply influenced by their contact with them. Paul says that the secret of their friendship is the fact that many of their interests overlap each other. "Discussions range from Dr. King to car maintenance, from politics to bird watching, from theology to economic inequality, from pacifism to long journeys in the US, from children and grandchildren to the Civil Rights Movement. You just don't easily end a conversation with Harky; there is always something yet to be said, a detail to add, and all that with his characteristic wittiness and broad smile."

Harky, "When I resumed my studies, I went to a big peace demonstration in Washington DC. against the Vietnam War. As usual, I sat in the front row with my tape recorder. Dr. King came right to me and asked, 'Harcourt, how is your study going?' That was the last time I saw him alive."

On April 4, 1968, Dr. King was assassinated.

Harky relates what he did the day before the attack on Dr. King. "Somehow, I had succeeded in getting one of Dr. King's closest staff members, Dr.

James Bevel, to come to Yale for a lecture. The next day I heard that Dr. King had been killed. Annelies and I immediately went to Atlanta to help organize the funeral. I was responsible for the coordination of the television broadcast."

At the request of Mrs. King, a recording of King's last sermon was played during the funeral. In it King says that during his funeral, there should be no talk of his awards, but only of his deeds: that he fed the hungry and cared for the poor. That he did not live in vain if he lived for justice. Ralph Abernathy, his closest colleague said in his speech, "They have slain the Dreamer, but not the Dream." Harky and Annelies stayed in Atlanta for two weeks and then went back home to New Haven where Harky graduated in May.

Harky then rejoined the staff of SCLC.

The Poor People's Campaign

Dr. King did not restrict himself to social and political issues but also gave attention to economic problems. The SCLC wished to be in solitary with all poor people, black and white and other minorities in America. They started the *Poor People's Campaign* in fall of 1967. The goal of the campaign was to get everyone a guaranteed annual income. To dramatize this at a time when Congress was spending billions to get to the Moon, poor people planned to come from all parts of the country on mule wagons and go to Washington DC. and camp on the Mall in front of the Capitol. When Dr. King was killed, they set forth to do the campaign. That summer they went to Washington DC. They called their tent camp *Resurrection City*. Harky was the link between the SCLC and the National Council of Churches.

Resurrection City was demolished by the police later in the summer. Harky and Annelies returned to Atlanta. There he became increasingly involved in the peace movement. In the spring of 1969 Harky was ordained as a minister in the United Church of Christ.

The SCLC came into financial difficulties, so in the spring of 1969, Harky and most of the rest of the staff was laid off.

—4—

The Street Has Many Faces

IN FEBRUARY 1969, ON the same day that Harky was laid off by the SCLC, Annelies found out that she was pregnant. The Klinefelters had no employment compensation. What to do?

Starting in September 1969, Harky taught psychology at the Kennesaw Junior College in Marietta, Georgia, for half a year. He was fortunate to be able to substitute for a sick colleague. In his contract he had to sign two things: (1) he would uphold the American Constitution, and (2) he would declare that he was not member of the Communist party. He did so, but brought a contradiction to the attention of the application committee: in the Constitution, freedom of associations is a right. Harky enjoyed teaching.

House of Harky and Annelies in Atlanta, Georgia, 1969-1972

During that one semester, Annelies and Harky moved. They had lived in an apartment close to a park for a year, but the contract was not extended because Harky would not promise that no blacks would visit them! Harky was by chance on the other side of the park when a "for sale" sign was put up on a house. It wasn't too expensive and consisted of three floors. Harky and Annelies decided to buy the house and to rent out the top and ground floors. The rent would pay for the mortgage.

Hippies and street people

In those days, Atlanta called itself a city "too busy to hate." Economic activity was more important than racial differences—an attitude that was an exception in southern US. Atlanta was the only place in a large area where black people had any economic possibilities. That climate could also tolerate the hippie movement. Atlanta became the center of the Flower Power culture in the southeast of the US. It all began very idealistically: hippies opposed materialism, bourgeois mentality and the lack of freedom in society. But the movement quickly attracted people who thought, "Easy money. Everything is free." This meant that, where hippies gathered, there were always street people.

Many teenagers ran away from home. For the young teenagers it was a means of attracting attention; for the older ones, it was often an escape from maltreatment or from an ultra- right upbringing. Harky was concerned about these teenagers. For example, he tried to help them reconcile with their parents in a way that allowed the teenagers to return home without loss of face. A young couple with a baby who was living on the streets moved in with the Klinefelters for a few months. Harky gave them his study, and the baby slept in a drawer of his desk!

Harky's involvement with street people coincided with the wishes of some local churches who wanted to do something for them. Andrew Young (one of King's colleagues, the first black Congress member from the South in nearly a century, former Ambassador of the U.S. to the United Nations and mayor of Atlanta twice) wrote a letter of recommendation for this project.

The Life of Peace Apostle Harcourt Klinefelter

Southern Christian Leadership Conference

334 Auburn Ave., N.E.
Atlanta, Georgia 30303
Telephone 522-1420

Martin Luther King Jr., *President*
1957 - 1968

Ralph D. Abernathy, *President*

J.E. Lowery, *Chairman of the Board*

Andrew J. Young, *Executive Vice President*

TO WHOM IT MAY CONCERN:

    The transient youth of Atlanta represent a direct challenge to the church. They have abandoned the security of middle class Southern culture because they are too sensitive and idealistic to accomodate its racist ideology, its empty ceremonial religiosity, and the viscious class exploitation upon which this culture is based. They flock to Atlanta on a pilgrimage of idealism; naive perhaps, and exceedingly vulnerable, but there is no denying their search for "a more excellent way" and the "abundant life"

    Often they are side tracked by drug and sexual experimentation and maybe are destroyed emotionally in the process and give up the search, but this is largely because we as Christians have been too threatened by their freedom and challenge to "preach a relevant word of good news".

    Harcourt Klinefelter and his young wife have felt this challenge and responded to the call to minister to this creative and confused sector of our society. "Harky" has an excellent background in the civil rights movement and has worked directly with SCLC for the past four years. This practical experience and his academic training give him an excellent combination of skills for this ministry.

    I sincerely hope that our churches can sense the urgency of this work and commit both spiritual and financial resources in this direction.

Sincerely,

Andrew J. Young

AJY:kc

Three national denominations, Harky's own church, the United Church of Christ, and the United Presbyterian Church and the Disciples of Christ,

The Street Has Many Faces

set up a project called *The Ministry to the Street People*. In 1970, Harky was commissioned to work with the hippies and street people of Atlanta. In his contract it was stipulated that the churches would pay him for three years. He wanted this more than becoming assistant minister to Daddy King. This new challenge fitted with his enterprising character. In this new position, he was called "Reverend Harky." The transition was quite logical: the hippie and peace movements are rooted in the Civil Rights Movement. On Saturday evenings, the police drove around to make drug busts. If a person was caught with a joint, he or she could get a two-year jail sentence. Actually, hippies were against using hard drugs, but not all street people were.

Harky, "On Saturday evenings I went to the jail where the hippies were detained, to encourage them and to make sure they did not immediately choose to be released on bail. They were better off waiting a few days, because they would otherwise have to pay the same amount again if it came to a court case. Sometimes, if they requested it, I gave them a Bible."

His work with the street people brought Harky into contact (and sometimes into conflict) with all kinds of authorities.

Harky also cared for the homeless. Long before professional mediation was commonplace, Harky was using the skills which he had learned in the SCLC Dialog Program in his work to promote reconciliation between the runaway teenagers and their parents. He organized medical care. He also set up a workshop space where the street people could sell such things as posters, candles and sandals in order to receive some kind of income. Later others carried on Harky's mission. The home started by the Salvation Army for homeless women to prevent this vulnerable group from getting into prostitution, still exists. A welfare organization continues mediation between runaway teenagers and their families.

Harky is very satisfied about the developments of permanent help for the vulnerable. He saw them as examples of one person lighting a torch and passing it on to someone else.

During a visit to one of the hippies, Harky was arrested for the first time. He knew he would immediately be released if he identified himself, but he decided not to do so. He wanted to experience himself how bad the conditions were in the city jail. He immediately called a radio station to speak in a live program to tell his story. "I am Reverend Klinefelter, and we are busy improving the city jail situation. Now I am here myself, and would very much like to describe the situation." Harky always remained the PR-man!

Harky also looked into and documented the displacement of hippies from urban neighborhoods. Blockbusting (See Chapter 3.) was not successful in getting people to fear that their house values would decline if hippies were to move in. The hippies did not threaten homeowners. Soon in Atlanta, there began to be strange fires in urban houses. Then the lots were "rescued" by realtors who offered them to builders of expensive offices and retail space. Thus, both house-owning urban dwellers and hippies were displaced.

Turbulent times

Harky, "Although my wife was sometimes homesick, it didn't enter our minds to go live in the Netherlands. This was the life! We had an average of six people for meals. The young people with the most urgent problems stayed with us, in my study. If you can help, you just do it. The only private place in the house was our bedroom."

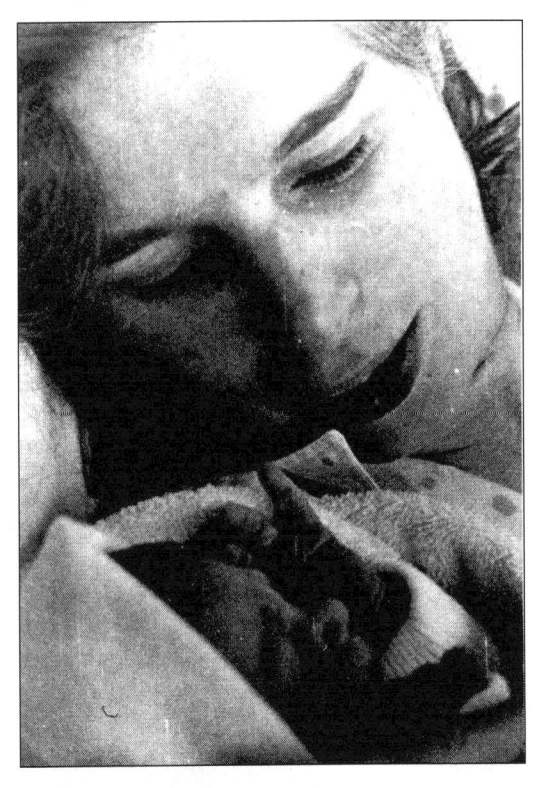

Annelies with Thea Lucia, Atlanta, Georgia, 1969

Annelies talks about that period, "It was a turbulent time with little privacy. When our daughter Thea Lucia was born in November 1969, I turned most of my attention to the baby. As kindergarten teacher, I wanted my child to grow up in peace, tranquility, and regularity. Those circumstances were often far from available in our house at that time."

The couple who rented the top floor was active in the peace movement and played an important part in the resistance to the Vietnam War which had been going on since 1955. They also grew marihuana. They quickly threw the bags of marihuana out the window when the police came to the door one day. It appeared later that the police only wanted to ask if the music could be turned down: the neighbors had complained . . . The ground floor was rented by Sleepy, an intelligent but illiterate hippie who often stayed in jail for short periods. The prison staff tried teaching him all kinds of things, but no one thought of teaching him to read and write.

Leading such a life was not without risks for Harky. After one demonstration, Harky was followed by a car. A gun stuck out of the window. The boy who had threatened him was later arrested by the police. His mother pleaded for him at the trial. Harky requested leniency, and it was granted.

Annelies' greatest fear was the Harky would be imprisoned, their daughter taken from them and that she would be sent home to the Netherlands. Upon reflection, Harky shares that feeling with her. "I have always felt safer in the Netherlands where weapons are illegal, soft drugs are legal. In America it was regretfully the other way around!"

Thanksgiving in Atlanta

Harky, "When we lived in Atlanta, there was a free pop concert in the park near our house every Sunday. A colorful figure, named "Bongo" because of his extraordinary appearance, cooked a large pot of brown beans and passed it out for free. There was a box into which donations could be offered. With this money he paid for the food for the next Sunday."

The last Thursday in November is Thanksgiving Day. This day is usually spent with a large festive meal with the family. Because the Pilgrims shared their harvest with the Native Americans, it is custom to place a basket with a turkey, the traditional meal of the day, on the doorstep of poor people. Most of the hippies, who were often without shelter, would go to their family or friends to celebrate. Bongo said he'd serve brown beans in the park for those who had no other place to go. It was an unexpectedly warm day. We had expected twenty or thirty people. Suddenly there were many people, about three hundred. How were we ever going to have enough food for all these people? A half empty stomach would only increase loneliness. And then a turkey appeared, and not long after, another one, and another one. Before the day was over, 23 turkeys had been brought. We celebrated later on at an youth center with the leftovers!"

It appears that the Miracle of the Feeding of the Five Thousand can be repeated in our times.

On Sundays Harky organized church services in his home. Such a service had no specified liturgy. There was much room for the contributions of visitors. Indian Joe was one of the visitors. He sold the left wing paper, *The Great Speckled Bird*. One day he came to Harky carrying a large Persian cat. "Reverend Harky, is my cat tripping?" he asked. He found that his cat was behaving strangely. Harky saw the round pupils of the cat and stated that it was definitely stoned. Harky advised, "Just let him be for twelve hours, and he'll be all right." Luckily that was the case.

Harky with hippies whom he married, Atlanta, Georgia, 1969

In his time as hippie-pastor, Harky performed a number of marriages of which several were definitely not performed in the standard form. Once he married a couple who pledged their vows in pantomime. First they both drank a glass of water, then a glass of wine. This was to symbolize Jesus' first miracle at the wedding in Cana where water later turned into wine. Many of these marriages are still going strong, and Harky has still contact with some of the couples.

Two stories by friends from the Atlanta period

Don and Judy Bender are good friends of Harky and Annelies, having worked together with them in Atlanta. They also offered shelter to teenagers who had run away and did peace work. Don recalls that he met Annelies in 1965 when he came to Atlanta and moved into the Mennonite center where she stayed. Harcourt came there often to see Annelies. They became friends. Even after they were all married, they kept close contact with another. Don describes the hippie movement as being unorganized and states that working with hippies required much flexibility. He says, "With Harky, life was unpredictable. Exactly this adventurousness made him perfectly suited for working with the hippies who would have nothing of a regular life!"

Skipper and Mary Marshall are also good friends of Harky and Annelies. Skipper says, "When I met Harky, he was no longer employed by SCLC but still involved with it. He and Annelies were good friends of Coretta King. Harky was working as pastor, his work being financed by several churches. His work was in building up the community and peace work. He brought me into contact with Hosea Williams, leader of demonstrations of the SCLC, and I was hired as a staff member to help organize demonstrations. When I was let go, Harky helped me to become part of the staff of the radio program *Dr. Martin Luther King Speaks*. I worked there twenty years as a producer."

"Harky married us in his backyard. Those were the days of youth and excitement, and Harky was a leader in the nonviolent resistance. He also found it his task to help young people to try to find a goal in life. For this goal, he sometimes offered temporary shelter. Harky did not have a large ego, but he had great influence and enjoyed much respect in the community."

The Life of Peace Apostle Harcourt Klinefelter

Hosea Williams, Carl Zitlow, Harky with Thea Lucia on his shoulders.
Mayday demonstrations, Washington, DC., 1971

Demonstrations against the war in Vietnam

During the period from 1969 to 1972, when Harky was a hippie and street people pastor, there were many demonstrations against the Vietnam War. The community organizing skills, which were basic to SCLC's fieldwork, Harky now applied to his work with hippies and the street people. In the bundling of the different organizations concerned with peace and justice at the time of rising anti-war sentiment, Harky organized the *Atlanta Alliance for Peace*. Together with Hosea Williams, one of Dr. King's colleagues, he organized the first march in Atlanta. About three hundred people joined the march.

Harky could now put into practice things he had learned from Dr. King. He taught demonstrators how to solve conflicts in a nonviolent manner. This could be accomplished in several ways. Harky was especially good at lowering the flash point during street demonstrations when incidents of injustice might lead to righteous indignation, anger, and possible riot. He was able to transform negative emotions into constructive actions. If a demonstration were to be successful, people needed to be trained to know what to do if they were attacked. The normal reaction when somebody is attacked is to attack the attacker. If this occurs in a demonstration, the friends of the attacker would most likely come to help the attacker. In the shortest time, there is a full-blown riot, which is the last thing demonstrators want.

Harky says, "What we did when somebody was attacked, instead of attacking the attacker, we would throw our bodies over the person being attacked, thereby spreading the blows. An example of this was an incident which saved the life of Rev. Andrew Young, one of King's staff. In St. Augustine, Florida, Andrew was attacked during a demonstration by a racist who planned to bash his head in with an iron pipe. Willie Bolden, a young *Freedom Rider*, ran up and threw his body over Andy's head. He caught the blows with his back and shoulders. Other people threw themselves over Willy and Andy. Thus, the violence aimed at one person was absorbed by several people."

The protests against the war in Vietnam began when David Miller burned his draft card in Central Park, New York, on March 31, 1966. It cost him five years imprisonment. The protests climaxed in 1971, with the *Mayday* demonstrations (a wordplay on "Mayday" = "SOS"). In the spring of 1970, there had been a nonviolent demonstration at the *Kent State University*, Ohio, during which four unarmed students were shot and killed by the National Guard. Then it was decided that, the next year on May first, we are going do as Gandhi did and sit in the middle of the streets in the Capital, saying, "If Washington won't stop the war in Vietnam, we will stop Washington." The call was answered by 10,000-20,000 people, the largest nonviolent civil disobedience action ever held in the U.S.

Trainings for and actions during Mayday–May 1971

Harky met with several experienced nonviolent activists and trainers to make plans. The purpose was to let the demonstrations be held as nonviolently and effectively as possible. A training team of about thirty people was formed. It was decided that the team should meet ahead of time, train the demonstrators in nonviolent action, and perform a series of protests themselves with trained people. This was to show people how nonviolent protests are carried out. In this manner, participants would become experienced and be able to help others. Mayday itself should be the climax.

The first activity was a demonstration in which wounded veterans, some in wheelchairs, returned their war medals. One person even returned the Congressional Medal of Honor, the highest honor and one only the president himself is allowed to give.

Harky, "A part of our plan was a demonstration at the Draft Bureau which was responsible for military conscription. The draft cards were sent from this office. The plan was to have small groups visit workers who were responsible for sending the conscription cards on a planned day, and to talk to them about the significance of their work. This plan was approved by the responsible authorities. On the chosen day, we were unexpectedly denied entrance to the building. While a negotiation delegation was allowed inside, the rest, about two hundred people, decided to hold a sit-in outside.

When the officials tried to go inside, they had to push their way through the crowd, and things threatened to get out of hand. To calm things down, I lifted my 1½-year-old daughter up and placed her on my shoulders. I preached a short sermon to urge the demonstrators to remain calm. Our only intention at that moment was to be present, not more. The further course of events shows the power of nonviolence.

There was a tiled path leading to the door above which we put a large picture of the Mi Lai Massacre bearing the slogan: 'If Washington won't stop the war in Vietnam, we will stop Washington.' (My Lai is the place in Vietnam where on March 16, 1968 American soldiers slaughtered civilians, many of whom were women and children). It was agreed upon that we might sit on the grass as long as we did not block the sidewalk. There were different possibilities: only sit on the grass and do nothing further, or stand arm in arm in front of the door. The latter was risky because, during training, it became very clear that, in this position, it is very easy to kick someone in the crotch. I had thought of a third option, a kind of human carpet. This method was chosen (See below). We thought that we would achieve our goal this way, calling upon the conscience of the workers and trying to move them to lay their work aside."

"Human Carpet", Washington, DC., 1971

The human carpet

Harky explains, "The carpet was to be composed of two groups of people on either side of the sidewalk. The row closest to the sidewalk would lay down on their stomachs alternately, their heads resting on their crossed arms beside the feet of the person next to them. Their faces were turned aside, facing the workers. The people in the rows behind them leaned over them, resting their crossed arms on the shoulders of the persons lying there. In this manner it was possible to see all the faces. This is an important point because it was an effort to improve communication in a protest aimed at the humanization of a situation. Eye-to-eye contact is important if one wants people to be seen as humans. One of the characteristic aspects was the willingness to suffer. An important point of the protests is to demonstrate that pacifists are not cowards."

The work of the recruitment officers caused pain to others, but they themselves, sitting behind their desks, do not feel the pain. The demonstrators wanted them to experience how it felt to cause pain by letting them walk over them. A declaration of this statement was repeatedly read out.

Harky, "The police did not arrest us at this time, not even when a postman with a bag full of registration forms for conscription did not throw it over us, but put it back on his shoulder, made the peace sign and left. Eventually the police did arrest us, of course, but only those who had come onto the path. Every time that someone was taken away, the place was taken by someone from the row behind. When someone was removed, we sang, 'I'm on my way to the freedom land. Won't you come with me?' Finally, there were only a few women and children left. I was wearing my clerical collar and was recognizable as a minister, and a Jewish boy was wearing a yarmulke. We were the last ones to be taken to jail.

Harky with clerical collar, Washington, DC., 1971

When we entered the prison, we heard that a number of workers had gathered money to pay our bail. We refused the money because we wanted to be solidarity with the hundreds of poor people who were held in custody for months because they did not have enough money to pay bail. After a day we were released against our will, in the middle of the night, because someone had paid bail after all.

The result of the action was that a number of officials of the recruitment office resigned their jobs and gathered money to support others financially if they also resigned their jobs. When an adjunct head of the office resigned, he organized a picnic for the conscientious objectors and co-workers. They showed a film in which soldiers told of their crimes against humanity."

Shortly before the climax on *Mayday* itself, Harky was one of the thirty people who trained thousands of demonstrators in small groups. The mass *Mayday* demonstration was a huge success.

Harky, "Thousands of people were arrested and held in stadiums or in the open air. There was the fear that a state of emergency would be called. The next day we wanted to give a press conference in the park near the White House: *The People's Press Conference*. But, if two or more people gathered, anywhere, they were immediately arrested. I suggested that the demonstrators should walk alone on streets close to the park until one o'clock. Then they should all go to an appointed place. It worked. At 1 pm, about 2000 people appeared!"

In the afternoon of the day of the people's press conference a demonstration was planned in front of the Department of Justice. The problem was how to get people to go from the park to the Department without being arrested. Harky succeeded in dividing the people into groups of 16 (4 rows of 4 people) and sent them on their way. The Justice Department was situated on both sides of the street, and people could be trapped if the street were blocked from both sides. During this demonstration, the police began arresting people from both ends of the street. There was also a group of Evangelicals with an American flag. Harky says, " I saw a megaphone in one of the backpacks and said to the demonstrator: 'The Lord needs this megaphone, may I use it?' He said, 'Yes.' Then I announced through the megaphone: 'If you are a good Christian, form a prayer chain on your knees around the fringe of the crowd'. They did so, and the chain held. The police decided not to use tear gas or clubs. Finally, everyone was arrested and pictures were taken of the demonstrators. There were police agents who sympathized with us and purposely put wrong names under the pictures."

During the demonstration, Harky married a demonstrating couple. They were the last to be arrested and spent their wedding night in jail! Harky was also arrested, and when he was released he found out that Annelies had also been arrested while listening to a senator on the steps of the Capitol—something not at all illegal. Eleven years later she received compensation from the government.

When Harky tells these stories, you can feel his enthusiasm. He still marvels over this, saying, "The creativity that you are handed from above is unbelievable!" He believes in a wider application of nonviolent techniques.

The *Way of the Cross* must be regarded as a counterpart to the *Way of the Sword*.

- The *Way of the Cross* means standing up against injustice with only spiritual armament of Love, thus risking your life as Jesus did.
- The *Way of the Sword* means sowing death and destruction with physical weapons to make people afraid in order to dominate. The *Way of the Sword* has been used on a very large scale for centuries, especially in situations of war.
- The slogan of the *Way of the Sword*, "Political power grows out of the barrel of a gun".
- The slogan of the *Way of the Cross*, "You can't kill an idea with a bullet."

Harky, "Through the years, the 'Way of the Cross' has mostly been seen as something that can only work on an individual level. Yet Gandhi, King, and Mandela proved that it can be applied on a much larger scale. Love is stronger than death. Dr. King said that love is an antidote to fear. If you are no longer afraid of being wounded or killed, your oppressors cannot subdue you. That is why Dr. King said: 'We have a power that is mightier than the atomic bomb. A bomb can only destroy. Only love can change an enemy into a friend.' Through these experiences I have become convinced that nonviolence can be applied on a much larger scale, even internationally."

Harky regards the human carpet as his best tactic. The carpet does not block the path, but confronts the consciences of people who see others visibly suffering. Harky knows of many examples in a variety of situations where nonviolent demonstrators were trained in the technique of the human carpet, not only through himself but also through other people. He says, "That others have adapted this technique is the proof that it works."

Move to Europe

This very fruitful and hectic period of Harky's life came to an abrupt end. Financial situations did not allow for the project ministry to the hippie and street people to be continued. At this time, because of a deep recession, the churches received less money and cut back on their social projects. Harky tried to find work as a minister but did not succeed. He returned to the SCLC as soundman, but only for a short period.

Harky, "My wife was in the Netherlands for her sister's wedding. I called her and said: 'Maybe it's time to continue my studies'. I sold the house and as many possessions as possible and went to England. I was accepted in Bristol University to do my PhD on Dr. King and nonviolence but could not get a scholarship. I tried to find work as a minister there, but that was very difficult." Because of church mergers, there was now an abundance of ministers.

In the summer of 1972 Harky, Annelies and little Thea Lucia moved in temporarily with Annelies' parents in Drachten, the Netherlands. They though that, surely some day there would be a church vacancy in England.

—5—

A Lifetime of Learning

WHEN HARKY LEFT AMERICA in 1972, he did not intend to emigrate, but to continue his studies in England and then return to America. That year, the *World Council of Churches* held a conference in Cardiff, Wales: *Violence, Nonviolence, and Social Justice*. During this conference, Harky talked to the head of the theological studies department at the University of Bristol, England. He received permission to work there on his PhD with a thesis on Dr. King and nonviolence. But there was no money and no job. So the young family, including 2 ½-year-old Thea Lucia, moved in with Annelies's parents in the Netherlands. Living with Mom and Dad (*Heit en Mem*) caused no problems; Harky got along especially well with his father-in-law. They weren't well off, but they managed. But it was meant to be a stop-gap measure. By the time their second child, Douwe Harcourt, was born in 1973, they had their own house.

A Lifetime of Learning

Annelies's father with baby Douwe Harcourt, Drachten, the Netherlands, 1973

While in the Netherlands, Harky continued to look for a job as a minister in England, but without success. Finding suitable work in the Netherlands was very difficult since Harky couldn't speak Dutch well enough to function as a philosopher/theologian. It appeared that factory work was one of his only options, so he got a job at the Philips factory in Drachten. He had to work swing shifts and earned only the minimum wage. It was also a difficult workplace. Here he personally experienced class discrimination. The assembly-line workers had a cafeteria with loud music and bad food, while the bosses had a comfortable quiet one with good food. Not surprisingly for an educated intellectual, his work making shavers was stultifying. He had to shout above the noise in the machine hall if he wanted to talk to a fellow worker, which he did in a mixture of Dutch, Frisian, and English. Having a large-print English Bible saved him. He was able to clamp it near his machine and read it while doing his job. He basically read it cover to cover. His boss never made a comment. Next, he read the Bible in Dutch with a dictionary beside him. Finally, he even had time to read some of the books that he never had the time to read during his studies.

Harky at work in the Philips factory, Drachten, the Netherlands, 1973-1975

In 1974, Harky gave his first training in the Netherlands with the *Fryske Fredes Freonen* (Frisian Peace Friends). The fifteen participants were all potential conscientious objectors. Several wished to demonstrate for the release of the conscientious objector, Kees Vellekoop. His request to be officially recognized as a conscientious objector had been denied, and he was sentenced to prison for twenty-one months. At a certain point, the participants found themselves in an overcrowded room. Annelies had been taking care of the meals and their two children and was not happy about the training taking place in their living room. When someone asked her for cutlery, she agitatedly threw it on the floor in the middle of the group. This was too much for the emotionally irritated participants. The training content had been quite confrontational. As Harky tells it, the group exploded, and it took a while to calm everyone down. Using this as an example, Harky taught them how to handle tension, a lesson that turned out to be very *a propos* for their demonstration in front of the prison in the city of Leeuwarden in support of Kees Vellekoop. The police were very unfriendly and kept pushing the demonstrators. For some moments, it looked like some people might not stay nonviolent. The training-group participants had learned about how to handle stress situations and influenced the rest of the protesters, and the demonstration did not get out of hand.

Main building "Overcinge", Havelte, the Netherlands, 1975-1986

Working at an adult residential consciousness-raising center

In the summer of 1974, Harky got time off from the factory work to be a guest teacher for a summer course in the adult residential consciousness-raising center in Havelte, the Netherlands, called *Overcinge*. For one week he coached high school students who were going to America as part of an exchange program. After this course, he was offered a permanent position at Overcinge. As far as Harky was concerned, this was just in time; he would not have lasted much longer in the factory. At this point, the Klinefelters moved to Wilhelminaoord.

By coincidence Harky had previously become acquainted with an American independent adult residential consciousness-raising center in the hills of Tennessee, the *Highlander Research and Education Center*. Harky had visited this center several times and had interviewed its director for the radio program *Dr. Martin Luther King Speaks*. He was quite impressed with the work done there.

Highlander Research and Education Center

In 1932, Myles Horton, being inspired by the Danish adult education movement, started a unique private adult consciousness-raising center in Tennessee. Its goal was to bring black and white people of the southern states together and to create a space where they could start to work together. This was before the Civil Rights Bill of 1964 was passed. At the time, such integrationist activity was against the law. The Center became the cradle of the Civil Rights Movement. Rosa Parks, Martin Luther King, John Lewis, Ralph Abernathy, Eleanor Roosevelt and many others took part in the programs provided by the Center. Folksinger Pete Seger put the song *"We Shall Overcome"* to music while there. The main goal of the center was to empower individuals. Ultimately the Center impacted Rosa Park's decision in Montgomery, Alabama, not to give up her seat in the "Colored Section" to a white person when the "White Section" was filled. This was the beginning of the Bus Boycott, the Civil Rights Movement, and the fame of Dr. Martin Luther King.

As to the course content of the Center, learning by experience is fundamental. Inductive learning (from practice to theory) rather than deductive learning (from theory to practice) is stressed. The goal of each course is to make people think for themselves, to make them appreciate other standards and values, to empower them, to help them break out of the denominational, political and, cultural boxes that have led to segregation, and to promote equality and democracy.

Harky as a course leader

At Overcinge, colleagues thought that Harky would learn Dutch quickly. This was too optimistic. The director, Simon Vuyk, recalls, "Harcourt would always express himself very poorly in his newly learned language. Courses brought no change or improvement whatsoever. The language barrier seemed to exist especially for his colleagues, who constantly tried to help him. The students remarkably had little problem with his language. Harky's enthusiasm, personal attitude, his richly filled suitcase of course materials, and his experience in the Civil Rights Movement were great assets."

The director at that time, Dr. Simon Vuyk, puts it like this, "One Saturday morning I met a group of students, who actually should have been home already, cleaning up one of the rooms. When I asked why they hadn't gone home, they replied, 'We cannot leave all this mess for Harcourt to clean up by himself.' No other instructor received such a reaction. In just one week, helped by his guitar, he was able to create a warm bond among people and draw out the best in them. A concerned but somewhat eccentric teacher is very attractive."

Harky is mentioned in *Adult Education in the Netherlands: 1925-2010* (Hilversum 2013). It states that the new colleague, Klinefelter, with his experience in the peace movement and wide repertoire of exercises, was a definite asset to Overcinge.

What did the Overcinge courses look like?

Overcinge played an important role in Dutch life. People came for short courses and boarded at the school. Forming a 24/7 community was integral to the learning experience. Even in a course as short as a week, people could get to know each other quite well. Life together also naturally taught some of the basic principles the school intended to stress. For instance, equality was one of the core values of the school. The students all had to help with the dishes. Perhaps more significantly, the kitchen staff ate at the table with the students and was included in some of the class' activities.

In a typical Dutch general course at Overcinge, people from all walks of life—from diverse regions, ranks, classes, levels of education and responsibilities— came together for one or two weeks. Core themes were family, education, society and work. Harky recalls, "To promote discussions we used role play, resource people, films and excursions. At the introduction meeting, we tried to create a feeling of safety. For example, participants paired up, interviewed and drew pictures of each other, then presented each other to the rest of the group. Only if people feel safe, can they open up for fruitful discussions."

No two groups were the same, but each short course (usually a week long) followed the same pattern. The first day the participants were somewhat reserved, observing the situation. The second day they were surprised at how quickly they were able to make some friends. On the third day, irritations started to surface. On the fourth day, role-playing and practical work was scheduled. This had two purposes:

- To learn about work situations and work relations.
- To learn that it was better to have quarrels break out during work than to unconsciously let them play a role during discussions.

Usually quarrels were quickly solved, resulting in the formation of a close group. The last day was for evaluation. In the evening there was time for deep discussions or simply for participants to enjoy their last hours together—and for some to mourn, knowing that the group would be dissolved come morning.

Rollplay, Havelte, the Netherlands, 1975-1986

Role playing during practical work

Harky explains how the practical work was intentionally organized, "The group chose two team leaders. The leaders alternately chose people for their team. We did whatever needed to be done: chopped down trees, laid a new tile path, or cleaned up rubble. When the job was done, we evaluated how it had gone. Here we also discussed how the role play differed from their own real-life work situations. Participants discovered that a highly educated boss didn't know everything and was often poor at doing physical work. Depending on the task, some "lower echelon" people took leadership roles. How and why this happened could then be analyzed at the discussion sessions. Frequently, the working men or women had clearer insights about what had transpired during the work session than did some of the other participants. At that time in the Netherlands, profit-sharing was a current topic. Should part of the profits of a company be shared with the employees? If so, should a lump sum or a percentage of the profit be distributed? Harky recalls, "I created a new situation connected to the role play in practical situations. Tables had been set for supper. One table was reserved for the group which was designated as having made the most profit, the other for the losers who had not made any profit. The winning team was seated at a nicely set table and received a whole sausage and a large portion of vegetables and potatoes. The losers sat at a bare table and received half a sausage, and significantly fewer vegetables and potatoes. You can image what happened. All hell broke loose. Then there was time to openly discuss everything afterwards. First the emotions were expressed, and then people were encouraged to talk about what had caused their anger, and what they thought would have been more fair."

Interacting with local people

Frits Beets, who lived near Havelte, was an extremely conscientious total pacifist. He had been an engineer in the Dutch subsidized Postal and Telephone company (PTT). This company was contracted to work on the NATO bunkers where the atomic rockets were stored.

He was ordered to set up telephone lines there. This was against his conscience. Thus he quit his job. He and his wife then started the Hobbitstee commune close to Overcinge in 1969. It was one of the first ecological farms in the Netherlands. He lived on fifty dollars a month and wore second-hand clothing.

In 1981 Harky invited him to come give a talk on organic food, something that was quite uncommon at that time. Nettle soup and parsnips were on the menu. Some students decided this was a part of the course they could skip and went directly to a Chinese restaurant for more familiar food!

Sometimes Frits Beets would come to Overcinge in the evening and share his poems and his way of life with the course participants.

Next to the Hobbitstee was a hyper-modern farm with computer-governed milking equipment. The dairy farm's efficiency meant that the family could earn a lot of money. They used some of their profit to adopt children in Sri Lanka, thus demonstrating that operating a high-tech industry and humanitarian concerns could go hand-in-hand. Students in Harky's classes went on excursions to both farms. Their experiences led to very creative and fruitful discussions.

Another local person who became involved in Harky's courses at Overcinge was a local mayor who volunteered to chair role-playing of city council meetings. After teaching about the variety of political parties in the Netherlands, each student was assigned to role play as a particular party member, preferably of a party he or she did not support in real life. This helped participants to see how democracy works.

Other excursions

Harky tells of taking a class to a demonstration. In preparation for leaving, the group had gathered together in the parking lot when Harky realized he had left a banner inside. He says, "When I returned to the parking lot, all the cars were gone. I had the permit in my pocket. What should I do? I went to the director's room, and Simon Vuyk offered to give me a ride. Later I wondered how many workers can go ask their boss for a ride to a peace demonstration?"

Watching film, Havelte, the Netherlands, 1975-1986

Films

Films, and later videos, were important tools to make participants think, for example, about their upbringings. Harky says, "We showed films on liberal upbringing and experimental schools. I showed propaganda films from both NATO and from the East Block. The only difference was that the missiles were pointing in different directions. The documentary on Dr. Martin Luther King, always made a deep impression upon the participants.

Individual attention

Harky was not only a teacher but a confidante to some participants. He recalled, "I paid attention not only to the whole group, but also to individuals. I invited people to join in discussions. But I did not press them. Once there was a young man who never said a word. On the last evening, he told me about his brother who had bumped against a sidewalk with his bike, had fallen off, and was run over and killed. From that time on, the young man had never spoken in public because he stuttered badly. And yet, he wanted to speak to the group the next day and thank them. We made a plan. There was someone in the group with whom he had become friends. We decided to put the two of them in the center of the group on two chairs. I said to the young man, 'Look into the eyes of your friend. Talk to him as if you were alone with him. The group will disappear into the background.' Would it work? Considering how important it was to him, I sat in silent prayer the whole time. While he sat there in the middle of the group, he stuttered a little at the beginning, but shortly began to speak fluently. People were very impressed. It was as though they had seen a miracle."

Smuggling religion

An instructor in a secular institution, Harky put questions on the meaning of life into the curriculum. For example, he would ask, "If you had the chance to meet the wisest person on earth, what would you ask ?" Or, "If a genie out of a magic lamp said you could make one wish, what would you wish for?" Or, "Which three books would you take along to build a new culture in a new world?" Or, "What would you like engraved upon your grave stone?" Or, "For whom or what are you prepared to risk or give your life?"

The following story shows that people can try to keep religion out of the conversation, but that it simply presents itself.

Harky said, "It was late in the evening during a course with the technical college students. We had had quite an intense discussion about abortion. The group consisted of rebel youth from the city and youth from very conservative churches. All the issues were brought forward: 'the mother should decide'; 'no abortion, not even if the mother's life is in danger.' Many students didn't think it a good idea to let an unwanted child be born. They thought the child would have a miserable life. One boy who had not said much answered, 'If I listen to you all, I must conclude that I should rather be dead because I was raised in an orphanage. But really, I have been happy my whole life!' Everyone was silent. The discussion turned personal, and the question was raised, 'What would you do if you found out that your fiancé was pregnant by someone else?' A remarkable answer,' My girlfriend and I are Christians. I am sure that she, just as I, would give the same answer. Even if it were well known that I was not the father, we would not only refuse abortion, but we would want to keep the child and love it dearly. We would say to the child that God was his father.' Suddenly I understood the Christmas story!"

Harky has a good knack of being able to carry on with mixed groups. Even if there is a large age difference, he is able to address everyone. His courses were very much appreciated, evidenced by the large number of his students who kept coming for reunions. His folder labeled *Nostalgia* is filled to bursting with thank you notes. One of the participants, Adrie, wrote July 4, 1980, "I thank you heartily for the efforts you made this week. You really do love the people and that is a must to come to a world of peace and justice." Arnoud wrote, "I have changed and become more critical." The pictures of those times show Harky with mustache and long black hair–still a little bit of a hippie–often wearing a vest, guitar within reach.

The anecdote concerning the human carpet in the church

During the Cold War of the 1980's, four Turkish Christians had applied for asylum in the Netherlands, but the Netherlands didn't want to jeopardize its relations with Turkey. At that point in time, there were Western rockets aimed at Russia situated on Turkish ground, so the West had to remain friends with Turkey. The Turkish Christians held a church service lasting 24 hours to prevent their eviction. As long as the service was in progress, the police were not allowed to do anything. Harky then taught those present how to form the human carpet that had been such a success in the Mayday demonstrations in the US. Harky was especially impressed by the fact that he heard the Turkish Christians pray the Lord's Prayer in Aramaic, the language that Jesus spoke. He had no idea that that language was still used.

Dream

Harky relates a dream he had at this time, "I was working at giving trainings, and I dreamed that I was in a large mansion. I discovered a hole in the wall of the basement. Further exploration revealed a space on the other side of the hole and a stairway. I climbed up and came into a room more beautiful than I had ever seen. To me this means that, if you sink deep inside, you discover unprecedented beauty."

During the Christmas course the holiday drink was decorated with the peace symbol, Havelte, the Netherlands, 1975-1986

A Lifetime of Learning

Peace Education

For Harky, another task at Overcinge was doing trainings in nonviolence. For example, he gave a course to Women for Peace, where he turned out to be the only man.

In 1979 and 1981 there were international trainings, both for those new to non-violence and those doing advanced training. These sessions were done in conjunction with the Université de la Paix in Belgium. Harky was able to adapt techniques he had learned in the Civil Rights and Peace Movements in America and put them into practice in Europe.

Portugese Bull Fight technique applied to another context

Using techniques learned in America and transferred to Dutch culture, Harky created courses for nurses in psychiatric hospitals. He started in Havelte and later continued in the training center of *Drieklank-Vredesveld*, Zeegse, the Netherlands. The so-called "Portuguese bull fight" was originally a method for neutralizing potentially violent activists. The method is called "separate with accompaniment" and is based on a principle used in Portuguese bull fights. The aggressive bull is not killed in Portugal but is returned to the stall, usually somewhere outside the city. In order to remove him peacefully from the ring, the bullfighters let a large group of cows into the arena to surround the bull. He now has attention only for the cows and can safely be led out of the city.

This technique can also be used if it seems necessary to separate one person out of a group. With the assistance of some nurse colleages, one nurse approaches the target person. From the moment that one approaches the person, it is necessary to talk to him/her. The objective is to create and maintain as much eye contact as possible. It also helps to keep repeating the name of the person if it is known, to present oneself, and to ask questions. In other words, do anything that keeps his or her attention. It must be very clear that the purpose is not to overwhelm, but to show attention and nearness. This should be made clear by choice of friendly words and tone of voice. If separation is needed the group of nurses surround the to be separated person and slowly move as a group to another room. Usually it is best to use a slow, gradual approach. The goal is to calm the person. It may not be necessary to physically remove the person from the situation;

it may be sufficient to let an aggressive person blow off steam and come to himself/herself. That can often make moving unnecessary.

Harky recalls, "We let participants practice this technique, but we were not sure it would work in actual situations. During a follow-up course, nurses told us that they not only used the technique successfully in their clinic, but also in a women's shelter. This technique is now included (without my permission) in a training manual for nurses."

Training based on the precept of the Portugal bull fight,
Havelte, the Netherlands, 1975-1986

Harky's work also included interactimg with like-minded institutions elsewhere in the Netherlands. He established contact with the Polemological Institute of the University of Groningen and the Peace Education Department of the Radboud University in Nijmegen. This resulted in round-table talks and provided very extraordinary meetings. Harky strongly believes that exchanges between thinkers and activists are very fruitful for the Peace Movement.

Bicycle repairman and the princess

One sunny day in May of 1981, Harky received a telephone call from someone whose name did not ring a bell. She asked if she and another woman could come to see him; she was busy with a project and wanted to talk to him about peace education. Naturally, Harky agreed to this. When the doorbell rang a few weeks later, however, he had completely forgotten about the appointment. It was hot, and he was home alone, fixing Douwe's bicycle, dressed in a pair of shorts without a shirt. Of course, he was embarrassed, but invited the women as graciously as he could to come in. He led them into the garden and raced upstairs to put on a shirt.

One woman looked familiar, so Harky asked her if they had met previously. No, she was sure they had not. Then she explained, "I am Irene van Lippe-Biesterfeld, and this is my secretary." Harky thought he would faint! Princess Irene was the sister of the Dutch queen Beatrix. Princess Irene told him of her desire to put peace education on television and wanted to take advantage of Harky's expertise. A good conversation followed, and Harky later visited Princess Irene's home in Soest. Harky and Annelies told their children, who came home from school and noticed nothing special, not to talk about this special visit! The television program was eventually made.

A black page in Dutch history and nonviolent action

From 1607 to 1949, the Dutch had a colony which is now called Indonesia. The Maluku Islands, famous as the "Spice Islands," were part of this colony. Some men from these islands became soldiers in the Dutch Occupational Force. When Indonesia became independent, the Malukan soldiers and their families were transported to the Netherlands. The Dutch government promised them they would make sure the Maluku Islands would become an independent state and the soldiers and their families would be returned to their homeland. This never happened. The Dutch did not make the Malukus independent before Indonesia became independent of Dutch rule in 1949, and modern Indonesia has no desire to make the Malukus an independent state. The Malukan people felt betrayed by the Dutch government and some young Malukans became very radical. In the seventies this resulted in several violent actions, a hijacking of a school and twice of a train.

Harky's involvement:

As members of the organization for active nonviolence, Harky and others volunteered in 1977 to take the place of the hostages who were being held by Malukans in a train hijacking at De Punt and at a school takeover in Bovensmilde. The members were willing to put their theory into practice. Others declared them insane.

Annelies knew that Harky was risking his life with this gesture but supported him. The nonviolent group was able to make contact with hostages and families of the hijackers as well as government people involved in finding solutions to end the hijackings. Just very recently, in 2018, Harky found out that the government had actually taken their offer seriously and had been in negotiation with the hijackers about exchanging a pregnant women with a replacement volunteer. Sadly, the hijacking came to a violent end. The Dutch government decided to storm the train and shoot some of the hijackers.

Later, Harky was able to make contact with both hostages and family members of the hijackers and other Malukans and to invite them to Overcinge in order to create a place where people could meet, share experiences and understanding between them At a later stage , some Malukans were hired as course instructors. For Overcinge, listening to and hiring Malukan course leaders was a step in overcoming the paternalism of the established order where the presumption is that the authorities know what is good for everyone.

Harky's goal was to explain and improve the situation of the Malukans. He also created space for Malukans to be able to discuss their political future.The Dutch government had made many promises to them, but had kept none of them. Because of his experience with blacks and whites in America, Harky could understand the Malukans' feelings of frustration and humiliation. During one of the courses, Harky received what he called the absolutely best reward he had ever received for his work and training. One of the participants read a letter from a Malukan family member who was in prison, who said, "If we had only come to Overcinge earlier, the hijacking would probably not have been necessary."

A Lifetime of Learning
The end of an era

In 1982, due to a change in the subsidy policy of the government, Harky's job at the center was threatened. Enthusiastic participants of his nonviolent defense courses lobbied on his behalf. They pleaded with the board and wrote a letter. One part said, "The strong spirit, involvement, and reflection needed in order to practice [a] nonviolent lifestyle and build this world, are greatly promoted and deepened through the peace courses taught in your Overcinge Institute. The central position which Harcourt Klinefelter takes raises the value to impressive heights. We know "Harky" as an enthusiastic man who dedicates himself to a task which he fulfills with integrity and love as a tribute to his mentor and exemplar, Martin Luther King." Harky's job was saved for a few years.

In 1986 the Dutch government took much more control over the types of courses offered at institutions it subsidized. Such institutions were now to offer more courses that earned them income. Harky was of the opinion that schools like Overcinge had originally been created to be affordable for people with little schooling who earlier in their lives could not afford to go to courses to promote democracy and that commercialization should not be allowed to undercut that original purpose. He therefore clashed with the new director who was seeking to eliminate unprofitable courses. Harky was dismissed.

Harky says, "I wanted a meeting with the director, which never happened. First I asked advice of the union representative, and finally, upon insistence of that person, I accepted the severance offer. I find it annoying that it went that way. It was not a fair game."

A book that records the history of adult education centers in the Netherlands says, "Klinefelter left Overcinge in 1986 because there was no room for his projects and working methods as a result of the new businesslike manner of running the school. He continued his work as an independent trainer." Simon Vuyk expresses it as follows, "Harcourt left the education center under pressure after working many years and with an impressive service record. Many participants and colleagues profited from his knowledge, his vision and his simulation games over actual problems."

Reactions of friends and colleagues from this period

A colleague, Bernard Robinson, writes that he and his former wife both worked in the Overcinge Center in Havelte. They came into contact with the Klinefelters while Harky was still working in the Philips factory. Bernard was impressed by Harky and by his work with Martin Luther King. A bond formed between them because Bernard had also lived in America for a few years. Being British-born, he also had difficulty with the Dutch language. Bernard was the person who told Simon Vuyk about Harky, resulting in Harky's appointment as an instructor in the Adult Education Center.

Bernard says, "Harcourt is sometimes long-winded, but at the end of his story there is always a pearl of importance. As far as I recall, I only discovered later that he was a minister. It never played a role in our relation. Peace and nonviolent resistance are universal themes, not only religious ones."

Bernard continues, "On his way from *Overcinge* to Havelterberg, at De Punt, with Malukans, saving me in a wind force of seven on the IJsselmeer or from a ravine in Dubrovnik . . . Enormous knowledge of man and nature, with humor and a guitar, 'a wandering minstrel,' and that all in the Dutch language."

When Harky received the royal award of the Netherlands in 2009, Bernard wrote an English poem:

Always a twinkle
Lurking in his eye,
Scattering diamonds
To every passerby.
From Atlanta to Appelscha,
From New York to New Buinen,
Let all know,
A human helter skelter,
A certain Klinefelter,
Is recognized today.
A Royal decoration is displayed,
A King's message is engraved.

A Lifetime of Learning

Harky receives a royal award, Steenwijk, the Netherlands, 2009

Ben Voulon, a course participant, writes, "At the end of the 70s, I received a telephone call from a Harcourt Klinefelter, whom I had never met before. He asked me if I, as a police officer, would give a lecture in the form of a dialogue during a course in nonviolent resistance. I was to talk to the participants about my violent experiences as an ME'er (member of the Dutch riot squad).

"When I first met Harcourt, I saw a man with eyes which showed intelligence and determined empathy, and which sparkled when he laughed. His heavy American accent gave him something special. Not that he needed that: I appeared to have met an ex-PR-man of Martin Luther King who had lost his great example, but not his ideals. During his job as PR-man he had undergone experiences which had formed but not deformed him.

I have never noticed any trace of cynicism in Harcourt. What especially appealed to me was that Harky appeared to be able to hold a mirror in front of the participants in his courses. He had organized a role play in which one half had to defend an imaginary embassy against the other half which had received the order to enter onto the embassy area with the necessary perseverance in order to hold a demonstration. The embassy defenders were armed with rolled up newspapers with which they could deal painful blows. During the evaluation it appeared that it had caused quite the commotion. I remember a couple which had lived in nonviolent conviction for years, but now, as demonstrator (wife) and defender of the embassy (husband), stood on opposite sides. In the evening the wife told her husband through tears how her husband had hit her in an unimaginable way, whereby it appeared that her soul was especially hurt. I saw Harky listening very quietly and observing the situation, and he later made a crystal clear analysis so the personal insight of the participants could grow.

Before the exercise, during my lecture about my actions with the riot squad and the dialogue following, I was understandably confronted by participants with their negative feelings about it. The exercise helped to transform the indignation they felt into a certain amount of mildness and understanding. That was quite a neat job. Harky was able to bring people with different interests and positions in society closer together.

Luckily I could also share less serious moments with him. I remember every detail of his juicy story about a sailing trip that could not take place because of his own unbelievable clumsiness. Probably this story sounded so close to home that I enjoyed it twice as much. Chaos can be a good foundation of creativity and you can certainly use some of that if you go through life as Harky does. I have experienced Harky as an idealistic humanitarian. A peaceful warrior."

Simon Vuyk, the Director of Overcinge, writes, "Harcourt had to earn a living and worked on the assembly line in the Philips factory making electric shavers. If needed, Americans have a broader interpretation of 'suitable labor' than we in the Netherlands. He was called to my attention. It didn't take long after our first meeting for him to join us in Havelte at Overcinge. Peace education in all its widest aspects was already on our program in the general courses due to the inspiring efforts of Arnout van Doorninck after the Second World War. He was about to retire. We badly needed Harcourt as his replacement to give the program a new and more concrete content."

Organizing, however, was not Harky's strongest suit. Simon says, "The story goes that Harky sat waiting for his students one Monday morning, but no one showed up. Later it turned out that the invitations to the gathering were still in the desk. No problem. This way, I became involved as an organizer augmenting Harky's practical work."

In Havelte courses were given to train people for taking part in large demonstrations such as the one, 25,000 strong, against the storage of nuclear material in the salt caves in Gasselte, Drenthe, in 1979 and the demonstration against the nuclear power plant at Dodewaard in 1980. Simon Vuyk also vividly remembers the effective technique that Harky taught the refugees who had taken refuge in a church. They feared a police raid. Harky had them form a human carpet that made entering the church impossible without walking over people."

Simon Vuyk continues, "Inventiveness and inspiration sometimes border on chaos. That is why Harky's life was one constant adventure. You would run into him in the oddest times and places. There were always absurd stories and events, like when his car was stolen in Alkmaar. The next day, driving elsewhere in the Netherlands, Harky saw his own car came up behind him and pass him. Harky promptly set up chasing it. Another time when Harky had parked in front of the Mennonite church in Steenwijk, someone broke into his car and broke off the steering wheel for some dark reason. These extremities were nothing compared to what he undertook as part of his calling.

After I left Overcinge, Harky gave a number of training sessions for workers in boarding schools for very difficult juvenile delinquents where I went to work in 1981."

—6—

Standing Side by Side

IN 1986 HARKY RELUCTANTLY left Overcinge because his courses were no longer going to be subsidized by the government as they had been before. He would very much like to have such a job again, but it was not possible. Everywhere there were openings for trainers, there were hundreds of applications. But he had to find work. So when in 1988 the Mennonite Church of Zeist, a town in the middle of the Netherlands, needed a minister, he applied. As a minister, he would also be able to work toward his ideals.

Actually, Harky found it a good idea to be able to work with people for a longer period of time than he did during his trainings. And anyway, he continued his trainings while he was a minister.

> **Service of Ordination**
>
> OF
>
> OVERTON HARCOURT KLINEFELTER, JR.
>
> TO THE
>
> CHRISTIAN MINISTRY
>
> BY
>
> THE NORTHERN NEW JERSEY ASSOCIATION
>
> OF THE
>
> CENTRAL ATLANTIC CONFERENCE
>
> OF THE
>
> UNITED CHURCH OF CHRIST
>
> †
>
> 7:30 P. M.
>
> FEBRUARY 23, 1969

Ordination as a minister

When Harky worked for the SCLC, he had not yet finished his theological studies. At a certain moment, Dr. King advised him to finish his studies because otherwise he would probably never do so. Harky is glad he did finish his Masters of Divinity degree, but he always points to the three times he was arrested in America, "I learned more about God and man in the three days in jail than in three years at Yale." He graduated in June of 1968 and on February 23, 1969, Overton Harcourt Klinefelter Jr. was ordained as minister in the United Church of Christ, in his home town church in Glen Ridge, New Jersey. Rev. Martin Luther King Sr. preached the sermon.

In his sermon, Dr. Martin Luther King Sr. emphasized how important the "lesser" among us are in God's eyes. He said, "Church people are willing to give water to Jesus, but not to the poor and the scum around them. Jesus can be found in all kinds of forms in our churches, but we don't recognize him. Never forget that, young preacher." He went on to tell the story of a woman who found the church door locked. She felt again, found it still locked, sat down on the step, and shot herself. The minister witnessed this tragedy and things changed within him and the church. King Sr. said, "Have a word of hope for everyone. Let people feel that they are worthwhile, that they belong. Make sure you never preach about anything you do not believe yourself. The world is in search of a story in which they can identify themselves. Try your best son, my dear son."

Daddy King and Rev. Grey at the ordination of Harky, Glen Ridge, New Jersey, 1969

Harky's sister, Lynn, writes, "I was moved and proud when Harcourt was ordained by Martin Luther King, Sr. because it accentuated the importance of his work for the SCLC."

Mennonite minister: the job

Harky went to work as a minister in the Mennonite Church of Zeist on April 2, 1989. Annelies was raised as a Mennonite. Harky and Annelies were married in the Mennonite Church of Drachten and became members there when they settled in the Netherlands. Harky felt at home in this congregation and became recognized as a Mennonite minister after studying Mennonite history. He did his first nonviolent training in the Netherlands in the Mennonite Church of Drachten.

Mennonites originated in Switzerland in the sixteenth century. There was a conflict in Zurich over adult and child baptism. Mennonites believed that a person must be of adult mind to decide to give his or her life to Christ. The city of Zurich set up a decree that forbade adult baptism. The conflict escalated so high that people were forced to recant if they believed in adult baptism. Refusing to do so meant they were a threat to the state and those who refused were sentenced to death or banned.

The movement spread through Germany and France to the Netherlands. In 1531, a Frisian, Sicke Freerks, was executed because of his belief.

Menno Simons, a priest in Witmarsum who no longer believed that bread and wine were changed into the body and blood of Christ during the Eucharist, was shocked of the death of Freerks and resigned his post. In 1537 Menno Simons was confirmed as the leader of the Mennonites in the Netherlands and northern Germany. He is the only Dutch Church Reformer. He taught people about adult baptism and let them write their own declarations of faith. He also preached about nonviolence and the separation of church and state. His followers carried no weapons, always sought to settle quarrels, and refused to swear the oath because a "yes" or a "no" was sufficient. All members were equal, could speak at gatherings, and could also perform baptisms and communion.

When the persecutions were happening in Europe in the sixteenth and seventeenth centuries, many followers fled to the States, especially to Pennsylvania, where freedom of religion was the norm. At this moment there are more then to twenty different branches of Mennonites, ranging from very conservative to liberal. The Amish are not typical mainstream Mennonites. Social activism is a norm in all the Mennonite churches.

Mennonites are especially concerned about the following:

- Militarism—Mennonites are usually conscientious objectors and also refuse to work or invest in industries that produce weapons.

- Discrimination—Mennonites are involved in abolition and civil rights movements, and object to police harassment of minorities.
- Poverty—Mennonites strive to support fair trade, thrift shops, and equal opportunity work
- Ecology—Mennonites engage in organic farming and organic medicine and use necessities, not luxuries, for daily life.

The Mennonites in the Netherlands are both theologically and socially very liberal. They perform same-sex marriages and are involved in all levels of activities related to the topics mentioned above. For example, the church in Steenwijk in the 1980s had a draft counseling office. It has also housed refugees, and for 25 years opened the doors at holidays for lonely people.

The Mennonite Seminary in the Netherlands was the first to allow women to study for the ministry (1905) and to be confirmed as ministers (1911). Since then many LGTB people have done their education and found a jobs as ministers in Mennonite churches. Many Dutch Mennonites have the plate on the wall with a saying which expresses the core of the Mennonite faith,

Wall plate. Text reads:
Baptize mature people,
Speak concisely,
Think freely about the Christian faith,
Deeds surpass words.

Theological principles

Harky never worked out his own theology systematically. He also never completely adopted the doctrine of one special theologian. Several sources formed his line of thought. In the first place, there is the Bible. Some people say that they believe something because it says so in the Bible. Others say something is written in the Bible because people found it to be true. Harky is closer to the second opinion.

For the formation of his theological thoughts, two people were very important to Harky: Jesus for how he lived and served God, and Dr. Martin Luther King for his admirable following of Jesus' command to love. King taught Harky that God is universal and uncompromising in His love. God's command is to love your enemies, the basis of nonviolence.

Besides the Bible, Jesus, and Dr. King, Harky was greatly influenced by the ideas of the Quakers. The Quakers believe that there is something of God present in everyone. The Holy Spirit (which they call "the Inner Light") can enlighten everyone, believer or not. Their thoughts on peace and justice are practical ones. Quakers help people on both sides of the line during a war. That fits with Harky.

Peace theology

Harky is active in Church and Peace, an umbrella organization of European peace churches and communities founded in 1948. Church and Peace is an advisory member of the Conference of European Churches and of the World Council of Churches. Harky was a board member from 2006 to 2012 and is still a member of the theological forum. Mari Noelle van der Recke, also a member of the forum, says of Harky, "As a member of Church and Peace, Harky has taken part in many conferences. He repeatedly refers to Martin Luther King and the civil rights movement. I find his stories fascinating. His experience in handling conflicts nonviolently once came in very handy. He was able to persuade a member who was about to quit to remain after all. I don't know how he did it, but the person did remain in the forum. When I asked Harky how he had managed that, he laughed like a boy who had snitched a cookie. I have very good memories of the beautiful trip I took to Croatia with Harky. We visited an inter-religious conference on the island Krk. On the way we had very deep personal contact. I admire how open Harky is about his personal experiences including those involving problems in the family."

Key questions for Harky

How does God lead people? God who knows everything, knew that at a certain time on a certain day the wind would blow so hard that the Red Sea would be dry for a few hours. That is why Moses came there at exactly the right time. God let Moses know that he had to hurry. To Moses it seemed as though God split the sea especially for him at that moment. For Harky this means being in prayer is very important, listening to the Spirit and act when the Spirit says act.

How should I share my bread? See the story about the hippies and Thanksgiving in Chapter 4.

In America and in the Netherlands our house has always been an open place for all people.

Shall I join the army? It was possible to discuss questions on conscientious objection in the peace office situated in the Mennonite Church in Steenwijk during the eighties. Later on, ways to deal with conflicts such as mediation were introduced by Harky in the Netherlands.

These questions constantly reappear in Harky's sermons and activities.

Installation service Mennonite Church in Zeist, the Netherlands, 1989

Preaching

During Harky's installation, the theme of the sermon was Ezekiel 47:1-12, a passage that means much to Harky. The river which flows from the temple stands for power that brings life. The theme of the sermon was petrified life versus living stones, and a watered-down life versus living water. The offering was intended for the Travel Fund of the Third World. Both the text and the intention of the collection demonstrate Harky's vision: a congregation which is alive and moving.

Harky's best sermon

In January of 1990, Harky preached in Zeist a sermon which he concerns his best ever. It was about forgiveness. The sermon, condensed below, was based on the story of Jesus' feet being anointed by a woman during a meal. His host, Simon, thinks to himself, "Jesus cannot be a prophet, otherwise he would know that this is a bad woman and not let her go on." Jesus says to Simon that he has received more love from this woman than from Simon himself. Her love is abundant and overflowing because her great sins were forgiven.

Harky said, "We see that Simon only thought of her as an example of her class. He reproaches Jesus because Jesus did not treat people as was expected. He thought that Jesus could not be a prophet because he did not treat according the existing standards. The effort of trying to limit God's love to our own circle goes on. One wants to see God as a judge who maintains the law and order of our social rules. He should order everyone to respect the rules of our club of so-called 'better people.' The opposite of this is a God who loves individuals with boundless love.

This is what we see in Jesus' reaction to Simon's words. Jesus didn't come to burden people with more rules. His manner is completely different. He saw people not as they were, but as they could be, and he treated them as such. Jesus broke through all the categories of pigeon-holing people as we tend to do. He reacted to the inner person. He looked more deeply at the women and reacted accordingly.

Simon thought that if he lived strictly according to the rules he would be perfect. Actually, by definition, rules are a limiting factor. The woman lived by spontaneously giving through love, and that is unlimited. She is forgiven because she has so much love. It is important to show love and forgiveness. If you love someone, you automatically do the things that help the other person or give pleasure. Simon merely followed the rules, but had little love. The woman broke many rules but possessed much love. Simon sinned little—and was forgiven little. The woman sinned much—and was forgiven much. 'We love because God loved us first.' Because we love we can forgive."

Harky is very capable of placing sermons in the proper perspective. He quotes a good joke about preaching, "If you don't hit oil in twenty minutes, stop boring." The message is clear: stop boring your public; don't preach for more than twenty minutes. He also adds that almost no one knows the names of sermons as they do of poems and books. He assumes that the reason is that sermons are connected with actuality and therefore limited in duration of their relevance. Harky judges his own sermons with a series of standard questions:

- Does this sermon encourage me to share my bread with my hungry neighbor, or do I just eat it myself?
- Does it contain something that is relevant to the moment?
- Does it contain something important in which I should believe?
- Does it make one think? A sermon should not prescribe the law but show the consequences of certain choices.

The Mennonite congregation of Steenwijk held a service in February of 2014 in which Harky played an important role. The service was prepared by the liturgy committee. Harky preached, and then the congregation divided into four groups to discuss discrimination by means of three questions.

- How am I discriminated against?
- What occasion made me aware of my own discriminating behavior?
- What can we, as a congregation, do against discrimination in our area?

There was a lively discussion, and people wanted to continue longer. Harky was happy to see this. He wants very much for people to be aware of discrimination, especially within themselves, and to take steps against it. He emphasizes that it is important to come into contact with the group about which one holds prejudices.

There are several themes for sermons which Harky often uses. One is compassion. When Harky studied in Yale, a fellow student committed suicide out of despair. Harky thought it ironic and poignant that fellow students grieved more about the assassination of Kennedy, which happened about this same time, than about the death of this student that no one paid attention to. Harky regards this event as one of the most defining moments of his life. He gets agitated about indifference. People often suffer more from indifference than from maltreatment. It resulted in his becoming deeply aware of the gravity of indifference and the necessity of compassion.

Innovative services

When Harky lived in Wilhelminaoord, he worked with the Mennonite Church in Steenwijk to organize alternative church services on Sunday evenings. The people sat around a low table on which were newspaper clippings, songbooks, the Bible, and other material. The participants would contribute stories/experiences which were important to them and would inspire others. Each time the theme was prepared by two volunteers from the former session. These services continued for several years after Harky left for Zeist.

He never succeeded in starting this type of service in Zeist. Harky says, "To my amazement, I discovered that I could accomplish more through the church council in Steenwijk that from the pulpit in Zeist." He did introduce a special innovation in the services in Zeist by using slides and even a computer and a projector. During the Peace Week in 1989, a peace tree was planted. Those present could hang paper cranes, a peace symbol from Hiroshima, in the tree under the watchful eye of the mayor.

Lena-Lynn is held up by mayor Rudi Broekhoven
to hang paper cranes in the peace tree, Zeist, the Netherlands, 1989

Language struggles

Harky taught himself Dutch through the book *Teach Yourself Dutch*. That was during the months before their wedding, after Annelies had left, and Harky was alone in America. He taught himself incorrect pronunciation, and his pronunciation never improved. He wants no help from Annelies; that only provokes quarrels. When Harky came to work at Overcinge, he had to do something to improve his understandability. He spent two sessions of two weeks in the language center in Vught, where he was drilled constantly. Considering his pronunciation of the Dutch sound "ui," one of the nuns who taught him considered him a hopeless cause. He is now on his tenth course with a speech therapist. It is typical of Harky who, even at eighty, refuses to accept a situation about which he is not satisfied. He is happy with the new therapist. She gives him lists of words to practice on. When he has a speech coming up, they practice the text together. She often listens to a recording of the speech afterwards. She finds that Harky is improving. He refers to the motto of Overcinge: learning is a life-time job.

It was quickly found to be necessary for Harky's sermons to be written out so they could be handed out to the congregation. This cost much time and effort, but the advantage is that he now has an extensive archive of sermons.

Pastoral care

Besides the innovative services and services on Sundays, Harky's task as a minister included pastoral care. Heleen van Noppen, Harky's secretary in Zeist says, "I made appointments for his house visits. This saved much time for him since he always engaged in lengthy telephone calls. Typically, Harky was always warm and sympathetic, but not always practical, and sometimes a little scatterbrained. He told the people of the congregation that they could call him at any time, and he meant it. I experienced this myself when my car wouldn't start one evening. When I called Harcourt, he came to help me immediately. He sometimes aggravated me too. I had no computer myself at that time, but could mail from his computer. That was very nice, but it usually cost me a whole morning because he couldn't resist showing me all kinds of new things on his computer. Usually, these didn't interest me at all. For Harky, time usually played no part in his work."

There are several kinds of pastoral care, and some are better suited for Harky than others.

Harky prefers to use *non-directive counseling*. This means that you only listen and try to let people find their own solutions. In time, Harky has adapted his visits and has become more direct.

Harky says, "Personally I find visits to *people with dementia* quite difficult. What can I say that still registers and can mean something to them? I always find it a painful sight to see people like that. I find it so degrading that one has to be like that at the end of his/her life. During my studies I usually did mostly church services. I have not had much experience with pastoral care with older people and this has made my work more difficult."

In cases of *terminal care*, the partner and eventually any children are always included in the conversations. Harky says, "Sometimes I could use my skills as conflict mediator in cases where the family relationship was not good and they wished to clear the air before the sick member died. I always was glad to be able to perform this kind of pastoral care. I felt I could really mean something for people then."

Harky continues, "*Problems in relationships* often crossed my path within and outside the church. I often coached interactions between parents and children, especially with teenagers. I had learned these skills while working with the hippies in Atlanta. Divorces often occur and are always dramatic and time- consuming for pastors to deal with. All the skills I ever learned, such as bonding communication, coaching, dialogue conversations, conflict mediation, and searching for creative solutions are then necessary. Follow-up care for all parties, including children, is very important. I have learned that a pastor should stay in touch with divorcing people, even though this takes months or even years of attention. After a divorce is finalized, my experience is that there are always scars left over and they hardly ever completely heal."

Pastoral care in crisis situations

According to Annelies, Harky was (and is) more of a teacher than a minister, but he stands strong in pastoral care in crisis situations. He finds it difficult to stay in contact with the demented, but if he receives a telephone call from someone considering suicide, he goes right away. If someone is doing better again, he stands back.

Harky, "Under pastoral care in *crisis situations* I understand a situation in which an immediate visit is called for. This kind of guidance suits me. I enter the room, look over the situation and, first of all, try to do what is necessary in all possible calmness. Sometimes it is necessary to call a doctor or ambulance; sometimes it is necessary to get people into a chair or make eye contact so that someone can calm down. I always try to stay with the situation until a solution for the problem is found.

Aftercare is very important in these cases. Pastoral care in crisis situations often becomes long-term care, sometimes months, sometimes years. I still visit someone whom I helped during my first year at Overcinge. He was schizophrenic, and I still visit him in or out of hospital care."

"*Suicide attempts* are something else. They require the immediate care of a physician. I have been asked to do mental coaching after an attempt several times. It requires a multidisciplinary approach. I have to work separately with many different parties. Sorrow, guilt, mental incapacity, shame, trust, are all possible subjects. It gives much satisfaction if a person can face life again."

Spiritual counseling

Harky, "During mentoring, I talk with a person about his or her spiritual growth. Many young people I had met at school contacted me later with respect to vital questions."

Harky regards it as rewarding and one of his most important tasks to help people discover what they can do or be and then coaching them on how to make their options a reality. One example is the story of Jolanda, a transgender woman, who visited the summer exhibition in the Mennonite Church in Steenwijk with her partner. She asked Harky if she might play the organ. That was allowed. Subsequently she often visited the services and other activities of the church. Ultimately she became a member of the congregation and now sits on the church council. She preached a few times in Steenwijk and is now studing to be a pastor. She now preaches often in Steenwijk and also in transgender churches. She has really developed in the last few years. Harky says, "I consider her my pupil, and she calls me her mentor." Jolanda says of Harky, "I find him to be a very special person. The saying, 'Still waters run deep,' definitely applies to him. I can always call on him with questions I have, and we often have beautiful, deep discussions.

He is also very widely orientated in faith and a passionate worker for peace and justice. He, together with Annelies, are an enrichment to my life.

He has told me about his peace work in former Yugoslavia and that he still profits from what he did there. I see that in the film *Selma*, too, which results in many requests for Harky to speak all over the country."

Harky preaching in Lexmond, the Netherlands, 2017

When Harky turned 65 in 2003, there was a large party with songs and sketches. The children had made a long chain like a tram strip card with all the special occasions of his life. Turning sixty-five did not mean the end of his work as minister and trainer. The pressure of having to earn money fell away, but other than that, not much else changed. Even now, at 80 years of age, Harky still preaches often Steenwijk, and elsewhere. During the night after the 65th birthday party, the telephone rang. A congregation member called to say that his daughter had made a suicide attempt. Harky went right to them. The daughter was admitted and treated. Fortunately, she recovered. Harky still keeps in touch and now even goes to the birthday celebrations of her children.

Working together with other religions

God's leadership is not reserved for one certain religion. In a sermon, Harky says, "Jesus proclaimed that God loves all people, good and bad." People of other religions are not excluded from his love. They can also believe deeply.

"If God is a God of universal love, I cannot believe that his message is limited to one certain religion."

Harky, "With respect to this subject I wish to say that it is important to propagate what your congregation stands for. In Zeist, the following took place. At that time we worked together with two other churches: the Reformed Church in Zeist-West and the Moravian Church. The three churches organized several peace gatherings. One of the speakers was a quite controversial priest, Kees Koning. I had invited him. He was known because he had damaged a F-16 fighter plane that was about to be sold to Turkey. He stayed with us several times and had become a friend. By inviting him to speak, questions on war and peace and civil disobedience were able to be addressed."

In Steenwijk there are broad interfaith services every year during the Peace Week, the third week in September.

The church as a movement, not as an institute

This is the title of Harky's thesis for his Yale Divinity School masters degree. He compares churches with coral. Coral is a living organism. In the beginning stages of growth, it is flexible. After a while the coral petrifies. It becomes hard and finally dies. This often happens with churches: first it is called a movement, growing and much alive. After a while the congregation becomes rigid and without passion. Power becomes an issue, and people want nothing more than to secure their positions. But power corrupts and inhibits change. If there is new growth somewhere (as is the case with new organisms growing on dead coral), then it is encapsulated by the existing institute or breaks away and begins a new organization.

According to Harky, new movements starting from time to time have a common denominator. He uses the term *apostolic succession of martyrs*. By "succession of martyrs," Harky means people who are willing to die for something they truly believe in, who would risk their lives through love for someone, and do so without using violence. Fellow supporters are inspired when one of their group is killed. Of course Harky recalls an example from the Civil Rights Movement. Jimmy Lee Jackson, a young black man who tried to protect his mother after a demonstration, was shot and killed by the police. Others came into action. The result was the march from Selma to Montgomery, Alabama. After Bloody Sunday, Dr. King called the clergy and others with good intentions to come to Selma. Rev. James Reeb responded to the call and was murdered by a racist. Harky was so impressed by this story that he decided to join the movement. Harky was called to help with the struggle for equal rights. The death of Rev. Reeb created a new life for him.

Martyrdom connects with the strong commitment of the Civil Rights Movement; Dr. King believed that undeserved suffering is redeeming. How great the suffering may be, the power of love is greater. Harry Belafonte said, "More people heard the message of Dr. Martin Luther King in the three days after his death than in all the preceding years."

How do you survive as pastor with all these questions thrown at you?

Harky, "You definitely need a personal sounding board, a stable home situation is desirable, and constant training is a must. It is absolutely necessary to keep doing the things that help you cope and charge your battery. It helps me to spend time in nature, to go bird watching and canoeing, to sit on a bench at the waterside and muse, to let my thoughts run freely, to cry or pray."

Harky says he prays often, but cannot say exactly why. He feels the need to be quiet, to listen to the Spirit and to hear what the Spirit has to say. Move as the Spirit says moves! What does prayer actually do? Harky points out that Mennonites have always been very modest about praying. He will never say that something turned out well because he prayed. And anyway, God knows what is good for someone, even without his or her prayers.

Coincidence or providence

God can use anything for good that happens. Harky believes that things that happen to a person, which are first experienced as negative, later can turn out to be positive. This is what happened when he left the church in Zeist in 1994.

Simon Vuyk relates what happened in Zeist, "Harcourt and Annelies were eminent, active members of the Peace Church. It profited royally from both their efforts. In spite of printed sermons in the services, Harky's poor pronunciation and insufficient knowledge of Dutch grammar were the reason that his contract was not extended after five years. Unavoidable?

Unfortunately, both the servant of the Lord and the church were not aware that dismissal would wipe out costly years of pension savings which had been built up during the years at Overcinge. Fortunately, I was able, together with some Mennonite friends, to find a way that allowed Harky to remain in the pension fund until his sixtieth birthday. For this we created a foundation, *PlusPunt,* which could use the expertise of Harcourt and create an income."

– 7 –

Working for Peace across Borders

NONVIOLENT ACTIONS CAN TAKE on different forms. Harky performed pioneer work with his efforts for peace both close to home as well as outside the Netherlands. He has a special antenna which senses which people, such as refugees or Muslims, currently are in the position of underdog. Situations which deviate from the beaten path give him energy. Wherever he sees chances, he uses his talents. He trains, mediates, and takes action.

the Netherlands

As of 1976, Harky and Annelies were active in the work group *Werkgroep Anti-Atoom Koppen Steenwijk* (WAAKS), an action group in Steenwijk against atomic warheads. This group organized a peace march from Steenwijk to Havelterberg every year on Boxing Day (1976-1986) There were nuclear warheads stored in Havelterberg at an American army base. At WAAKS' peak in the 1980s, some ten thousand people came together. Harky took care that everything went in an orderly fashion. In the newscasts that NOS-TV broadcasts made during the marches, one can often see Harky.

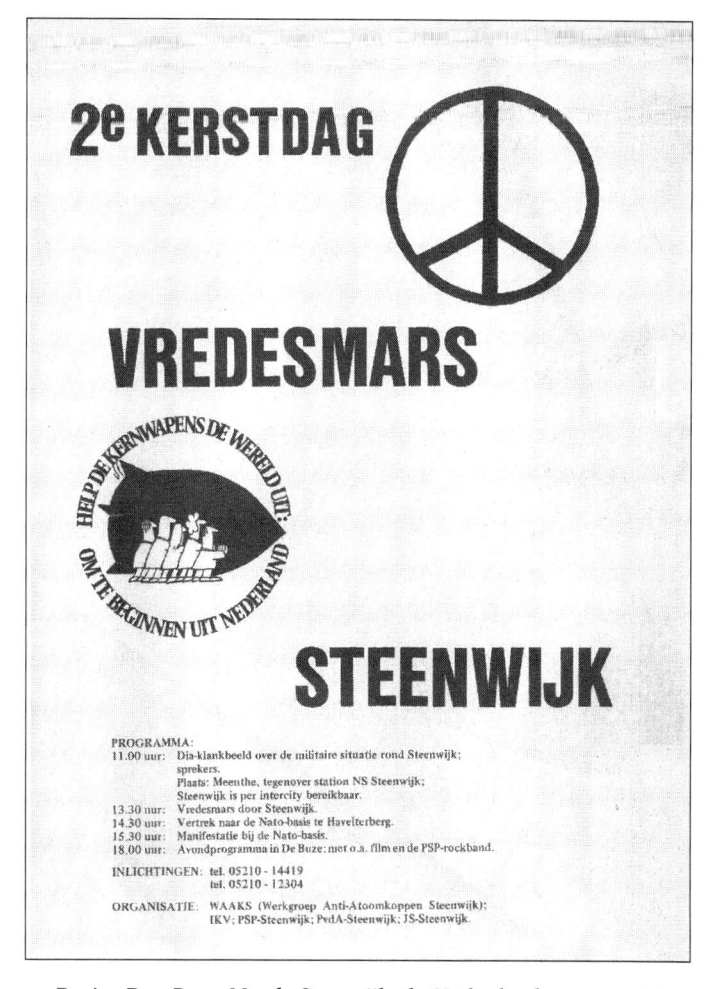

Boxing Day, Peace March, Steenwijk, the Netherlands, 1975-1986

Hans Hageman met the family in the seventies. He says that Harky and Annelies were active partakers of peace work from the beginning. His first acquaintance with the Klinefelters came by way of Annelies. She had offered to help when the WAAKS organized a flea market to raise money for their actions. Hageman says, "Using their large family car, we spent several Saturdays together driving criss-cross through Steenwijk to pick up all kinds of things for the sale. When participation of the yearly peace marches grew, Harky offered to organize a weekend of trainings in nonviolent resistance at Overcinge, where he worked. Using the available audiovisual equipment and with intensive discussion and action groups all under

Harky's supervision, preparations for demonstrations were sometimes a bit unorganized but reasonably effective, and above all sociable—typical of seventies training days. Also typical for Harky and Annelies was the great hospitality they offered in their home in Wilheminaoord where they lived with their three children. Meetings often took place there. Besides practical aspects they often had a contemplative and moral-ethical side that Harky brought in through his experience and knowledge."

During one peace march, young boys on motorbikes created a disturbance. When Harky met them, he started a conversation, admired their bikes, and took films of them which he could immediately show them, something special at that time. The boys never made trouble again.

In the US Harky had gained experience with demonstrations and in techniques to let demonstrations occur peacefully. In the Netherlands, he trained guards who were to keep matters under control. He was involved in the large demonstrations against cruise missiles on the Malieveld in The Hague on October 29 of 1983. For other action groups Harky was involved in training demonstrations at the atomic center of Dodewaard

In 2000 Harky was involved in the first Dutch training for nonviolent peace workers, an initiative of the *Association for Active Nonviolence, Hogeschool(College) Windesheim*, and the *Dutch Expertise Center of Alternatives for Violence*. Harky was also a member of *Physicians Against Nuclear War*, a Dutch organization for medical polemology, the multi-disciplinary study of war and peace. Every year he gave mediation training to this group. At that time, this was completely new in the Netherlands, and he considers himself a pioneer in this area.

Mi Za Mir: living together peacefully

Harky became involved in *Mi Za Mir* ("We for peace"), a peace movement which ex-Yugoslavian refugees who fled to the Netherlands formed in October of 1991. The group was comprised mostly of conscientious objectors, deserters and artists, all highly educated, who had fled the war.

Mi Za Mir kept in contact with peace movements in former Yugoslavia from its headquarters in Amsterdam. Their goal was to stay together because they wanted to work towards peace together.

Harky was impressed. These people lived according to the commandment, "Love your enemy." He came to Amsterdam several times to help support them. He was also asked to give trainings directed at nonviolent resistance. For these trainings, a group of nineteen Croatians, Bosnians, and Serbians gathered. Harky used all kinds of methods to encourage the participants to put themselves in the shoes of the other and to solve conflicts in such a way that opposing parties would not have to shame themselves afterward. When Albanians from Kosovo, Serbians and Croatians in refugee center close to Utrecht began to get angry at each other, Harky was called in. He went and took a Serbian and a Croatian along. Together the three of them managed to calm the situation down. The trouble had actually started because of misunderstandings due to language problems. Harky made sure that a news report came out saying that it definitely was not an ethnic issue that had caused the problem.

Refugee centers: conflict prevention and mediation

For the *PlusPunt Foundation* (1994 to 1999), Harky worked on solving conflicts and conflict prevention in refugee centers. He was inspired by the biblical commission to treat the stranger well. After twenty years he still talks passionately about it. "It was important to get the workers to place themselves in the situation and experience of the refugee residents. So many factors played a part: uncertainty about the future, fear of the unknown, traumatic experiences, language barriers, difference in origin and culture among the residents." It is worth mentioning that there were always constructive solutions to be found during the courses. PlusPunt was also used in times of crises, but preventing conflicts was more important. Conflict prevention and transformation skills should be one of the basic tools of the workers, Harky felt. It belonged to their equipment as much as a first-aid diploma. The first question a worker should ask him/herself should be: How can I approach this resident so that I can strengthen his/her dignity? Simon Vuyk talks about Harky's trainings in dealing with aggression and conflict in the refugee centers, "a critical group leaders in Overcinge valued these training highly. We made a plan, engaged a female colleague, and made offers to refugee centers. Workers and volunteers there were often confronted with aggression of traumatized refugees. It was desperately necessary to train them to understand the backgrounds and handle the outbursts of anger. Nothing of this nature existed. For this reason, an organizer and two trainers were able to offer many training sessions at a reasonable price. When our colleague, Anneke, found a more attractive job, Harky and I continued our role playing courses for quite some time. Then larger organizations woke up and offered much more expensive programs with situations being acted out by others instead of role playing by participants. Directors of the refugee centers preferred these courses although they cost more money. But we were five years on, and Harky's pension had been rescued, so we stopped PlusPunt."

Harky recalls that the trainers who had competed with PlusPunt hired professional actors to play the part of residents and that they only concentrated on conflict management. According to Harky, it is much more educative to let the workers play the role of residents. His trainings were aimed much more broadly than conflict management; they were especially focused on improving the communication between residents and workers. When the atmosphere improves, and there is no more talk of two camps with rival interests, residents can recover some of their independence and, thereby, their dignity. According to Harky it was definitely important to teach the workers effective techniques to be able to mediate and so prevent conflicts. He also paid attention to the many kinds of emotions of the workers.

NODAS

He also greatly supported the work of NODAS, Nood Opvang Dakloze Asielzoekers Steenwijk, an emergency shelter for homeless refugees in Steenwijk. From 2002 to 2016 this foundation found shelter for eighty people who could not find a home after their stay in refugee centers. All kinds of people worked in this foundation, churchgoing and those who were not. Harky tells the story of a meeting that was arranged with the councilman responsible for housing. Three ministers came to the appointment. NODAS had arranged that, during the conversation, a family of turned-away refugees would be dropped on the doorstep of the town hall. The councilman had to deal with this. He then arranged that they could be admitted under the care of the Salvation Army in Zwolle. NODAS was able to make a deal with the city council. Temporary shelter was arranged for asylum-seekers through housing corporations in areas that were to be demolished. When the refugee center in Steenwijk closed, the stream of clients dried up.

Working for Peace across Borders
Far from home; Outside the Netherlands
Working in Bosnia, Croatia, and Serbia

Harky regards the time he spent working during the war in ex-Yugoslavia as an important part of his life. War broke out in 1991 in ex-Yugoslavia. Slovenia severed itself. That happened quite peacefully. In the fall of 1991, though, the Serbs and Croatians began to fight. Years earlier, in 1986, Harky had given trainings in nonviolence in Dubrovnik, Croatia. Through this he was still in contact with the peace movements there.

The Dutch Interdenominational Peace Movement (IKV) and peace movements of other countries, in the fall of 1991, organized a peace caravan of forty buses to go from Trieste in Italy to Zagreb (Croatia), Sarajevo (Bosnia) and Belgrade (Serbia) via Hungary. About two hundred representatives of many nationalities went to the capital cities of the provinces of ex-Yugoslavia which were now separate countries. Harky went along as representative of the Dutch Mennonites. This peace caravan was meant to be oriented on the new war, to make contacts, and to support local peace groups and people searching for nonviolent solutions.

Sarajevo, Bosnia, 1991

In Sarajevo, which was not yet involved in the war, they held an inter-religious manifestation on the steps of the cathedral. Harky recalls, "I threw a paper airplane with a dove as pilot into the air there and said it was made by Dutch children at a peace conference. I told them that Sarajevo was widely known as the place where the First World War began, but that it was my dream that it would someday become a center for peace."

The miracle of bread in the bus

During the peace caravan, there was often no opportunity to buy fresh food. The level of frustration was dangerously high. Harky took the microphone and said he would like a repetition of the miracle of sharing bread that Jesus had done long ago. He had some meat and cheese and was willing to share it. Someone else said that he had some bread. Harky made a cheese sandwich and asked who would like one. Others said they had some meat, fruit and cookies. Harky walked along the rows and shared what there was. Juice and wine were passed around, too. There was more than enough. Someone started playing guitar and people in the caravan shared their folksongs with each other. Harky concluded, "We didn't serve four or five thousand, but we all had a sandwich."

Training in nonviolent action with refugees on the Dalmatian coast

In the summer of 1992 a German Mennonite Peace organization asked Harky to give trainings to the refugees in nonviolent actions. Harky was asked to work in this area of conflict because he had experience with inter cultural and mediation trainings. Harky recalls, "I knew about Yugoslavia and the cultures firsthand. I have seen nonviolence work on personal and national levels. I was convinced that active nonviolence would contribute greatly to reconciliation after a civil war. Not that I could reduce the loss of blood but a repetition of war in the long term could be prevented. Reconciliation after wars is very important. Another factor was the desire of people involved in the peace movement to support others who suffered violence because of their ethnic background. I believed that God, whatever happened, would do something good with my intervention. This belief gave me the courage to do this work." He divided his time among organizing, training, and pastoral care.

As of summer 1992, Bosnia became involved in the war. Bosnians and Croatians fought against the Serbs. Refugees were housed in hotels and camping sites on the Dalmatian coast. Then something happened that Harky still cannot understand. Bosnians began fighting the Croatians.

Entrance to the UNHCR headquaters, Vukovar, Croatia, 1993

Here are some notes from Harky's reports of his stay on the Dalmatian coast in the summers of 1992-1995. He says, "The land along the coast lies between high mountains and a sky-blue, crystal-clear sea. Every house literally has its own fig tree and fruit trees. It resembles Palestine and Israel. It is hard to imagine a more beautiful place. Together with another team member, I rented a room in a little village, with a balcony facing the sea. The inhabitants of the village were very nice, and when I was there, I often sat drinking homemade plum brandy with them. Fortunately we were situated close to Split with our team. We started every day with a short service, guitar music and open prayers. Everyone who was there at that moment was welcome to join. My task was to work with the people from the United Nations to make sure the refugees had enough time to decide where they would or would not like to go, and to help them with this decision. During the summer of 1993 Harky met the refugee, Diebe. She set up language courses for refugees in order to improve the contact between different groups of population, something of which the government disapproved.

Harky with refugees on the Dalmatian coast, Croatia, 1993

After refugees were evicted from Hotel Riviéra, I slept with them on the ground outside the hotel. There were no toilet facilities, and there was no water. During the night, neighbors brought water, blankets and food to the people. The refugees shared what they received, even with a police agent and an ex-Croatian soldier."

The Croatian government wanted to place different groups in different camps, separate from each other. Harky and his colleagues received briefings from the United Nations High Commissioner for Refugees (UNHCR) to hear what was happening where. This information helped them to find out how the circumstances would influence their work. This is how they knew that splitting up the refugees was being continued. The Croatians were placed in nice houses, with even TVs. The Bosnians had to be satisfied with primitive camps. On the border areas with Hungary, they often stayed in tents, even in winter.

The hotels where the Bosnian refugees had been staying were cleared because of the coming tourist season.

It is essential here to point out that not all people who say they believe in Christ are somehow involved in an international conspiracy against Muslims. That is why it is so important that our work is done with deeds—for example, living together with the refugees and sharing their fate.

Lena-Lynn and friend in a canoe on the bay in Markaska, Croatia, 1994

Not all of his experiences were negative. Harky holds fond memories of the music he heard there. "The Bosnian music is the nicest. It is Klezmer-like."

Later, in 1994, Harky, Annelies and Lena-Lynn went on vacation in Croatia and Bosnia. They enjoyed the Dalmatian coast and became friends with a refugee family. Lena-Lynn canoed with the son of the family along the river that opened up into a beautiful bay. There was a truce at that time, and it was safe. Harky remembers the coastal area as a fantastic place.

Refugees on the beach in Markaska, Croatia need food not weapons.
Harky sent a letter with these words to the president of America, Forth of July, 1993

Through his contact with refugees, Harky was invited to help with a training in Budapest for trainers from Croatia and Serbia. He remembers the following: at the beginning of the training, a Croatian gynecologist, Katriena Kruhonja, said, "I do not know if I can trust the Serbian women, Manda Prishing." However, they found a way to trust each other. After twenty-five years, Manda and Katriena still work together. They help refugees find new homes and give trainings across the borders.

The story of the lion

Many years later, Manda said that a story that Harky had told during the training still moves her.

"I looked toward the horizon and saw a lion coming directly at me. I was terrified. When it came closer, I could see it more clearly. I discovered that is was not a lion at all, but a large dog; a St. Bernard or something.

But a large dog can be dangerous too. The animal came closer still. Then I saw that it was not a lion or dog, it was a person. He crawled over the ground. He came closer. He appeared to be wounded. But then I could not see him anymore because he was hidden by shrubs. Carefully I approached the bushes and spread the branches. I looked at the man on the ground. His face was covered with mud and blood. I wiped his face clean. Then I discovered that this man, who I first thought to be a dangerous lion or dog was my *own brother*."

Interreligious training: helpful instruments for a peaceful way of life during and after war

In 1994-1996 Harky was involved in training the middle-level management of interfaith groups from different countries: Serbs, Bosnians, and Croatians. There were representatives of Muslims, Jews, Greek Orthodox, Catholics, and Protestants backgrounds. It was made sure that enough women took part, and not only the regular officials. The trainings were held under the umbrella organization of CSIS (*Center for Strategic and International Studies*), a think-tank in Washington DC, which advises the American government among others. The training team consisted of three trainers and John Paul Lederach as an advisor. Harky was the trainer with the most practical experience.

Preparations for the training took place in a luxurious hotel in Washington, DC. It was necessary for the team to become used to responding to each other and to set up a good trainings program. Harky went there several times and sometimes combined the trip with a visit to his sister, Lynn.

The first training was given in a former sport hotel in Osijec, Croatia. That was where the war between the Croatians and the Serbs, had started. The city was still surrounded by Serbs.

The program of the training

After an introduction, participants got acquainted. There was always sufficient time allowed for getting to know each other. Not only did these people come from different countries and belong to different religions, they also spoke different dialects. This was the first attempt to win each others' trust.

One initial activity was only done once, that of imitating each other as if in a mirror. The purpose of this is that a person learns to accept leadership and to know and trust each other on an emotional level.

This activity consists of imitating each other's hand movements.

The participants were deeply insulted:

- This was child's play and you don't do that with adults.
- Young and old do not need to look to see who the leader is because the young people will always look to the elder as the leader out of respect.
- Men do not play with each other in this manner.

This shows how important sensibility for cultural differences are. Harky was not surprised at the result. He had experienced this before with other international trainings.

When the participants began to feel safe, *dialogue* in mixed groups took place. In small groups, talking about one's childhood, feasts, births, marriages, and grief helped people to see each other as persons. Experiences and emotions were often similar. Discovering this helped people to be open with each other and trust each other. Harky used the experience he had earned in the civil rights movement with dialogue conversations. The final activity was to exchange war experiences.

Harky, "To bring the cultural differences into view, we did a word association exercise with the words *peace* and *conflict*. This was to learn from each other what these words mean in their cultures and what they mean to each person individually. We used the Bosnian word *mir*, which means the same as *peace*. For the trainers this word exhibited the positive meaning of peace with justice. The participants, however, had negative associations with this word. For them it meant 'peace at all costs,' or 'Stop fighting for justice.' Or, even worse, 'Just give up and capitulate.' After a series of conversations, we decided to use the word *peace* after all, and in the associations that the trainers had with the word."

After this it was time for the theoretical approach. *Mediation* was offered as a way to solve conflicts. After hearing the theory, it was practiced in role playing. During the training everyone had a chance to be mediator.

One of the principles was to look for a *win-win* solution. An example of a win-win situation is from the following story: Two factories need the oranges that grow in the district. There are constant arguments about them. Then they decide to enter into a discussion and the question is asked, "What do you need the oranges for?" One says, "I need the peel." The other says, "I need the pulp". By asking this question, the impasse is broken and a solution can be searched for which satisfies everyone's needs and provides peaceful cooperation. This story is used to show that asking creative questions makes a win-win situation possible. A conflict is not always what it appears.

Nonviolent communication was always a part of the training. It concerns using "I" instead of "you" when describing conflict, "I feel hurt" instead of "You are or are acting stupid." The principle is to express one's own feelings and not to project them upon the other. Talking together in this manner requires much practice.

Besides all these emotional and intellectual training activities, *spiritual food* was also necessary. There was a spiritual moment every morning and evening, prepared and held by the participants. It resulted in inspiring and surprising sessions. Since so many different religions were present during these trainings, it was good to learn each other's rituals, words, and songs. It is moving to discover where people find the spiritual strength to withstand war.

The training was also designed to let people talk about their war experiences in small groups. The participants constantly came to the conclusion that war was bad and that all parties are guilty of war crimes, not that the opposition was composed of bad people. After all, they had lived together in peace for centuries. There were many mixed marriages. People found it strange that their favorite place of vacation was suddenly now in a foreign land. There was mutual recognition on both sides.

Making peace

Harky talks about the training in Visico, a small village thirty kilometers from Sarajevo. "We stayed in a Franciscan monastery. It was a very special community, an unbelievable group of people. The monastery was on the opposite side of the river from the village. There was no glass in the windows, it had been replaced by plastic. To buy groceries we had to run quickly across the bridge out of fear of snipers. During the nights you could hear gun shots. During an evaluation session, we heard the story of a woman whom the Serbs had thrown into a concentration camp. There, she and her daughter were used as human shields. And what did she regret in the training? That the Serbian Orthodox priest was not present so she could forgive him. There were more stories of this level, stories about Muslims who risked their lives to help Christians and vice versa."

Harky on the training in Sarajevo in 1995

"We were to hold our training in Sarajevo in the spring of 1995. The United Nations only allowed you entrance if you had a helmet, a bullet-proof vest, and an invitation from the local authorities. This was during the height of the battles around Sarajevo, which was completely surrounded. The only place a person was more or less safe was the airfield. It was not sure whether the UN would want to fly us to that area. Even the night before, we kept hearing controversial news about whether the training would be on or not. My son was emotional and accused me of loving other people more than him. I answered, 'I am doing this for you because I want to try to prevent that you will ever come into the situation that you have to choose between killing someone else or letting yourself be killed.' Then he understood and let me go. Finally we received the telephone call. We could go!

Two Franciscan monks, drivers of the jeep to Sarajevo, Bosnia, 1995

To reach Sarajevo the training team had to take two jeeps, driven by Franciscan monks in the middle of the night and drive over Mount Igman, a high mountain above the city. On top of the mountain we had to stop and remove the brake lights for fear of being shot at. We could see all the stars in the heavens and also flashes everywhere–mortar fire, a hundred meters from us. We stayed in the Franciscan monastery in Sarajevo. The first afternoon sirens went off during our training. No one reacted. Why did no one go to the bomb shelters? The participants told us that mortars have no warning time. The sirens mark where the mortars have already landed. If they are not nearby, no one goes into a shelter."

Harky at the Franciscan monastery (with bullet holes), Sarajevo, 1995

"The training, which proved to be very successful, occurred during the period before the Orthodox Easter. It had been agreed with the UNHCR that we would be picked up directly after the training and before the Orthodox

Easter. This became impossible because of threats of new fighting. So now what?

The only way was to climb Mount Igman by foot because the road was under fire. It was close to sundown when we walked. I looked down on the city, and everything looked so peaceful. I could hear the nightingales singing. Meanwhile some mortars fell a few hundred meters from us. I had the cassette player open the whole time, to make a last recording for my family in case we didn't survive. But we did make it. These experiences changed me."

Harky(with helmet and bullet proof vest) on top of Mount Igman with Sarajevo in the valley, Sarajevo, Bosnia, 1995

Harky admits that these incidents were traumatic. He doesn't really have nightmares about them, but he did acquire a mild form of Post Traumatic Stress Syndrome. He hopes never to come into such situations again. But, he would do the same thing again.

Training in Serbia

After the training in Sarajevo, Harky was able to acquire a visa to train in Serbia. War was still being waged, and he had to travel via Zagreb and

Budapest to reach Belgrado. Like the journey out of Sarajevo, it was an emotional and tense one. He found it very important to also meet the Serbian clergy and people involved in the peace movements again on their own ground and take note of the situation in Serbia. Here Harky discovered that the refugees were not lodged in camps, but in private homes with families.

The last training for all participants from the three countries was in Hungary in 1996. Everyone had survived the war, sometimes just barely. Harky was happy to see all the people again.

The Peace Event in Sarajevo in June 2014

During the peace caravan in Sarajevo in 1991, Harky had thrown a paper airplane with a dove as pilot into the air with the wish that Sarajevo someday might be a symbol for peace. That wish was granted during the Peace Event of 2014. The manifestation made a large impression on Harky. According to him, the seeds that were planted during the war in Yugoslavia had grown into trees with many fruits. Twenty five hundred people visited the manifestation. There were one hundred ninety workshops. Annelies and Harky organized two of them. One hundred fifty young people camped in tents on the same grounds where the Klinefelters had their camper. They had many beautiful encounters with people working towards peace.

They were happy to combine this kind of trip with other events. This time they handed out packages in the flooded areas in Bosnia and Serbia and drove through beautiful nature parks in Slovenia and Austria on the way home.

Balkan Peace Team

Harky's trainings led to him becoming involved in the Balkan Peace Team which was busy with concrete activities which should contribute to rebuilding the states of former Yugoslavia. The team consisted of members of about ten religious and nonreligious peace groups from diverse countries of Europe. These participants offered support to local peace and human rights organizations.

According to Harky, ninety per cent of the people can live in harmony, and ten per cent make war. He heard the same comment in all three countries, "We can live in peace with each other; the politicians want war."

Egbert Wever, a friend from the Balkan Peace Team remembers Harky

Egbert Wever says, "The Balkan Peace Team, a peace project in Serbia, Croatia and Bosnia formed in 1994, brought me into contact with Harky. His practical attitude, his wide field of interest, and his humor made him a well-loved conversation partner. You do not see this combination often among people who are fighting for a better world. You have to be serious in order to persevere, but that often limits enjoying yourself. Harky does it. He works terribly hard toward a better world, continues for many years, and, in spite of all the wars and misery, manages to stay positive. If Harky comes over, he always has some kind of goodies along, like his own brewed beer, donuts or sandwiches. I enjoy contributing to one of his interesting projects or repairing the computer for him, having discussions with him, or cooking together. Time flies when we are working on computers, in discussion or cooking. Annelies often calls to ask where Harky is. He's on his way, but first has to round up a few things. I can understand Harky's mixture of English and Dutch. It was hilarious that Eric Bachman, a coordinator on the Balkan Peace Team and an American, asked me to translate Harky's story into English. We really were talking English at the time. Harky has often surprised me, Catholic-raised and now secular, with his interpretation of faith. I used to think that all Protestants regarded Catholics as heretics. It doesn't matter to Harky what a person believes. It's all about a practical interpretation. We share the motto: 'Working together towards a peaceful world where respect for the other is a central goal.'"

Christian Peacemaker Teams (CPT)

In about 2000 Harky became closely involved in the founding of CPT Netherlands (Christian Peacemaker Teams). This human rights organization was started in the mid-1980s in Chicago, USA, by members of Mennonite communities in the US.

The core idea of CPT is nonviolence as Jesus lived it. The organization is open for participation by people with diverse convictions and sources of inspiration. Important parts of the meditation sessions are praying and singing together, listening to each other, and sharing the sources of inspiration which give the participants the strength to go on, and even to love their enemies. Their aim is the reduction of violence, undoing oppression and the restoration of human relations. CPT only works where local groups invite them to help with bringing about changes nonviolently. A few dozen team members are paid for working in areas of conflicts and a small number of part time paid workers are stationed in the headquarters in Chicago. All costs are paid out of donations. People can be stationed, after an introduction course of a month, in a field team. It depends on the requests from the areas of conflicts and a person's own possibilities, where he or she will be stationed.

Harky at CPT stand at the National Liberation Festival May 5, Assen, the Netherlands, 2013

A friend also involved in CPT, Maarten van der Werf, about Harky

Harky met him when Christian Peacemaker Teams was started in the Netherlands. They have worked together often and for long periods of time.

Maarten remembers an incident with Belgian beer at a conference of Church and Peace in Heverlee, Belgium. "Harky loves Belgian beer and we had smuggled a few bottles inside in a plastic bag. The bag tore in the hallway to our bedrooms, so there was no longer any talk of secret beer..."

According to Maarten, Harky is faithful, good-hearted, amazingly creative, very knowledgeable and yet always modest. He is not someone who starts quarrels, but a reconciler, someone who is completely captured by the idea of nonviolence and his experiences with Dr. Martin Luther King.

"The expression *wait a moment* is directly connected to Harky in my opinion. This expression is often used to create a bit space for a Harky-action." Maarten has an example. Shortly before leaving for Germany—wait a moment—an extra jerry can with water had to come along. Harky had made a sunblind in front of the radiator which he could work by hand to regulate the cooling water.

Marten calls Harky's talent for fixing things proverbial. He does so with extraordinary ingenuity and especially with cheap materials. "I once received a birthday present which is an example of ingenuity and nonviolent action. Harky had fastened a clock to a parking disc so the actual starting time was always visible. Cheerful nonviolence!"

After a period in another country, it was always good to come home to be with family again.

—8—

Raising Courageous Citizens

THE TITLE OF THIS chapter has the word *courageous* in it while the reader might expect the word *mature* or *emancipated*. Harky and Annelies wanted their children to grow up to be emancipated and to be able to speak for themselves, but they also want them to speak for the voiceless and work on undoing opppression—a clear but not a simple goal. Now that the children are grown, Harky and Annelies think that their goal was achieved; the children think independently and are socially involved. They are ready to help where needed, try to empathize with others instead of judging them, and realize that the world is bigger than their own environment.

Douwe, Lena-Lynn and Thea Lucia as children, Wilhelminaoord, the Netherlands, 1981

A recurring theme in Harky's stories about his children is the conflict created by his being both a father and an apostle for peace. He strives for a good relationship with his children. He is interested in them, wants to know what interests them, and is open to their discoveries. But Harky also wants to work at peace, to be there where conflicts are escalating and intervention is are asked for.

Whenever possible, Harky took his children along to activities and demonstrations. There are pictures of Thea Lucia, at a year-and-a-half-old, in Washington, DC. during the *Mayday* demonstrations (1971), and of her at two-and-a-half years old, during a demonstration in Atlanta with a balloon carrying the inscription, "Make love, not war." Further on in the chapter are the stories of Douwe and the Boxing Day march and about Lena-Lynn and the women's peace camp.

When Douwe was twenty-two years old, he once said to his father, "You love everyone more than me." Harky replied, "I am doing this for you; so that you will never have to choose between killing or being killed." Endlessly having to choose, always thrown back and forth, seeing that you fall short, takes a lot of energy. Harky did not always succeed in combining good parenting practices with his peace work, but quite often he did. Following are some examples.

What Harky remembers about his children's first years

Thea Lucia was born in Atlanta, Georgia, in 1969. At that time it was very special for the husband to be in the delivery room. Harky and Annelies found a hospital that would allow this. Harky also took part in natural childbirth classes. Harky had not finished reading the textbook on childbirth when Annelies went into labor, but he wanted to help Annelies with the breathing techniques. Annelies remembers his calling out, "Not so quick! I am still on chapter three." At this time Harky worked with the hippies and the house was a refuge place for run-away teenagers. This situation was not good for taking care of a baby. Harky recognized the dilemma; after two months a safe house for young women was erected by the Salvation Army. A peaceful home for Thea Lucia was thus created.

While in Atlanta Thea Lucia would use her favorite toy, a walking giraffe bike, to head to the large playground in the nearby park. A few times Harky would have to search for her, because she was very quick.

Thea Lucia was two and a half years old when the family moved to Europe. Thea was able to speak English, Dutch and Frisian very well and knew what language to use with the different people in her surroundings. A memorable moment happened at the corner grocery store. People would buy there and pay once a week on Friday, payday. Thea Lucia once entered the store and "bought" some candy. When the storekeeper asked for money, she said, "Write it down, my grandmother will pay this on Friday." This only happened once, as you can imagine. On December 5, Saint Nicholas Day, the saint and his helpers would visit the house to bring in the presents. Afterwards Thea commented, "Saint Nicholas had the same shoes and voice as our neighbor." How attentive. It was the neighbor!

The second child, Douwe Harcourt, was born in January of 1973 in the Netherlands, and Harky was working shifts in the Philips factory in Drachten, a small city in Friesland in the northern Netherlands. It was hard to get enough sleep with a baby crying regularly in the home. At home we spoke English and Dutch. Douwe could not handle this mix of languages and began to stutter. Also Harky's Dutch was not very fluent. We decided to stop using English and to speak only Dutch in the home. When Douwe was a small boy, he and Harky made a bow and arrow. Harky taught Douwe to stalk animals. Douwe commented, "Indians are smart people; they can live without electricity."

In 1975 Harky got a job in a residential adult education center, Overcinge, in Havelte, a small town in the province of Drenthe, a bit further south of Drachten. This work suited him much better. The family moved to Wilhelminaoord, a small village close by Havelte.

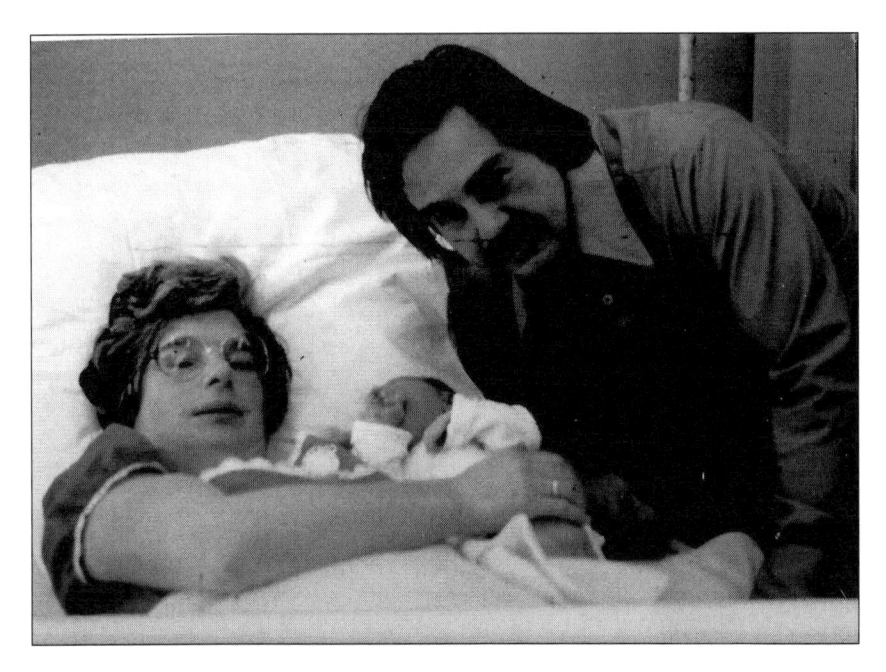

Lena-Lynn birth, Meppel, the Netherlands, 1979

Here their third child, Lena-Lynn, was born in November 1979. What does Harky remember about this? The delivery was very tense because the placenta would not release. Annelies threatened to go into shock. Harky was in a panic. Fortunately, they were in a hospital, and effective measures could be taken. Lena-Lynn, being the youngest, was often "the baby" in games played. She loved to play with dolls and carriages. Going for a walk with the dog and one of the parents was a great delight.

School age

Vividly Harky remembers that the children learned to ride bikes and to skate.

One day Harky was on his way somewhere with daughter Thea Lucia on his bike. She said, "I haven't whined for an ice cream cone all morning. Can I have one now?" She got one. According to Harky this was an example of the natural talent the children have of getting what they want in a very original manner. They have no power, so they must find another way. This is the way it should be more often: to think of a solution in a

Raising Courageous Citizens

creative manner instead of using power. (See Moral Judo in the Principles of Nonviolence appendix.)

Harky applied this technique of an appeal to the conscience to help his children in the following story.

The little children had made a wonderful snowman and came back inside. Later on, bigger children came and threw snowballs at the snowman. This hurt Harky, and he went outside. He said, "I can't forbid you, but I wonder if you think it's as much fun if you know that there are a couple of very sad children inside." The older children left laughing but came back a short while later to build an even more beautiful snowman for Harky's children.

Iglo in Wilhelminaoord, the Netherlands, 1978

Often Harky told the children the fairy tale called Kingbird, his own composition that was related to Martin Luther King. Because Harky moved to the Netherlands after writing the story, "The Kingbird and the Eagle" was never published in school books, as was his intention.

The Kingbird and the Eagle

Once upon a time there was a beautiful forest where many happy birds lived. They sang about the Father in Heaven who cared for them. They didn't need to build barns to store grain. There was always enough food because none of the birds ate more than was needed. One day an eagle came to the woods. Every day he stole a fish from the Osprey. Something had to be done, but what? Martin, the little kingbird, was the only one who dared to fly to the eagle. "Stealing is wrong, stop it," he said. The eagle became angry and flew after Martin. He picked at him with his sharp beak, and Martin began to bleed. The other birds came to help him. Martin said it wasn't too bad to become wounded if you were doing something towards a good cause because you would feel good inside. After a few days he flew to the eagle again and asked him to stop stealing. "You don't have any friends. If you start catching rats and foxes, the birds will become your friends." The eagle began to feel silly because of the little bird that kept pestering him. Martin, the little kingbird was the hero of the woods. The eagle and the Osprey became friends, and all the birds lived happily ever after.

If the children quarreled, Harky helped them talk their issues out so the conflict didn't get out of hand. There is a famous family story about Douwe who had earned his "drivers' license" in Legoland, an amusement park in Denmark. Thea Lucia let the certificate fly out the open car window. Douwe was inconsolable. Harky says, "I stopped the car on the side of the road and talked with the children. You can't just let something like this go by. It is a time when you need to teach your children that this kind of thing must be discussed. There has to be attention for the pain, pain that Douwe felt in this case."

Thea Lucia(1969)

Thea Lucia (1969)

Now that Thea Lucia has grown up, she writes the following about her father. "My father and I resemble each other. We do good and want everyone to feel good. We try with all our might, but often, to our disappointment, have to admit that it didn't work out. Realizing our dreams and ideals does not come easily.

As a child I always found it busy and turbulent at home. I never knew what was going to be happening. Were there three Ghanaians? A teenager in trouble? A meeting with fifteen people? A friend in tears who needed a shoulder to cry on? It was all possible, and it all happened. Everyone was always welcome. Stay for supper? No problem. We'll just add a sandwich. We share what we have. All very beautiful, but very disquieting.

It did, however, give me a much wider view of the world. I am glad that I came into contact with many different cultures. It made me much more open-minded. Strange things now don't strike me as all that strange, because I always judge a new situation by some moment in my childhood home. I developed a strong intuition as to how people and groups feel".

"Both my parents are very driven and enthusiastic about working towards a better world. Harky has a more global aspect, and Annelies is involved in the society around her. It is beautiful to see how they grant each other the space to follow their hearts to their goals. As a child I was not able to see this. I struggled to see who was there for me, for us. Other people's problems always seemed larger and more important. Emotionally I felt lost. It was also confusing that they both worked hard for peace in the world, but often quarreled at home. Luckily I was free to go into the woods. There I felt safe and supported and calmed down. Harky and I are similar in this. We feel very much at home in nature, and I am still thankful to him for all the things he taught me about nature."

"I missed having a father who was used to bringing up children and setting clear limits. Handling my emotions and frustrations wasn't my father's strongest asset. But I know he loves me. We are really deep soulmates. We both have a power source which helps us to do the things we believe in."

"As a person I find Harky special. He is a passionate and spirited man who dedicates his life for peace. He is concerned with the wellbeing of others and tries to help with large problems the world over. In the same way, he works with heart and soul that people and also Mother Earth may be healed. He works on a world-wide scale whereas I work from close by trying to bring people closer to their inspiration. I sometimes feel that I stand in the shadow of my parents. When they are working to help refugees from Syria on Lesbos, and I am working toward the development of a few people, I feel that I am falling short. But they do support me on my spiritual path and in my work. I received a holy pipe, a Chanunpa, from them and am now an official pipe carrier. The Chanunpa is indispensable in the rituals of the natives of America. Through using this pipe, I am even more connected to the North American background of my father. I smoke the peace pipe, and this completes the circle."

"I am especially thankful for the inspiration I unconsciously received from my parents through their way of living, and for their unconditional love and support."

Raising children for peace

Annelies reports, "What Harky found very difficult was to give preference to his children if someone else was in need. He was sure his children would be all right and focused on those he was not sure could manage. The children did not always experience this as support from their dad. In retrospect, he understands that Douwe was not happy with yet another demonstration of nonviolent conflict management, but rather wanted a father who stood unconditionally on his side!" One example is Harky's role in the following case. In Wilhelminaoord Douwe was not always happy with his friend, the village rascal. But Harky found that the boy needed more chances, even if it cost Douwe expulsion from some of his favorite activities. Among other things, Douwe was excluded from scouting because his "friend" had made a mess of it.

Harky recalls, "All our children have two nationalities: American and Dutch. One day Douwe and some of his 'friends' were at our house. They were running down foreigners. 'They should all leave the Netherlands,' they said. I sat down with them and talked about a society that includes everyone. Later I asked Douwe how he felt during that conversation. He said it hurt him how they talked about his father and indirectly about himself."

Lena-Lynn at the womens camp demonstration at the NATO base,
Havelte, the Netherlands, 1982

In the summer of 1982 all over Europe women set up peace camps close to US military bases where atomic missiles were kept. Close to the NATO base in Havelterberg, seven miles from Wilhelminaoord where Harky lived in those days, one of these women's peace camps was established. Annelies was closely involved, and during the summer months she and the girls, Thea Lucia and Lena-Lynn, spend a lot of time at this camp.

On Boxing Day, the children were taken along on peace marches organized by WAAKS. When Douwe was seven or eight, he made a banner all by himself. He used one of Lena-Lynn's diapers and painted the peace sign on it. He carried it along on the yearly march to Havelterberg. Harky is moved and proud when he thinks of this. Douwe often heard a click when he answered the telephone. Harky is quite certain that he was being monitored. Of course, the phone was wire-tapped, and yes, in response, he was restrained on the telephone. Sometimes a meeting place was changed at the last moment so the intelligence service could not be around in time to spy. Harky is very matter-of-fact about it. That's the way things are.

Taking the children seriously??

Harky could be insensitive to his children's safety as well as their needs. He regrets one incidence in particular. Everyone was welcome in the Klinefelter's home. When Thea Lucia was fifteen, a young boy who was homeless came to live with them. He fell in love with Thea Lucia. She wanted nothing to do with him and found it irritating that he kept staying with them. Harky took the boy's side. Later it appeared that the boy had stalked her and that she felt unsafe. Harky becomes emotional when he realizes that he missed out—that in caring for others he left his daughter in the lurch.

When Thea Lucia was in her twenties, she came back to live at home in Zeist. At one point Thea Lucia had a boyfriend who was using drugs. That caused quite a commotion. Harky had the tendency to take the side of the underdog (in his eyes). Thea Lucia wanted to break up, and Harky went to see the boy in jail. The rest of the family was not happy about it.

These episodes stood between Harky and Thea Lucia for many years. Finally they went on a canoe trip in Sweden for two weeks. They talked it all out and became much closer to each other.

Yet Harky did not usually repeat the same mistakes. When Lena-Lynn had a boy-friend who had become psychologically unstable after his military service in Yugoslavia, and he threatened her, Harky unconditionally took the side of his daughter and sent the boy away. Her siblings were very relieved at this, because they were afraid their parents would not intervene.

Being available for everyone at all times is not appreciated or understood by everyone. The children sometimes felt set aside because "the other person" went first. Listening carefully, talking and explaining endlessly, and not hurting his children for the benefit of another:

Harky learned it by trial and error.

Vacations

The highlight of the year was the camping vacation. The family mostly stayed in the Netherlands, but often also visited Denmark. They stayed away as long as possible. Besides the tent, the canoe always had to go along, fastened to the roof of the car. Vacations were often combined with demonstrations. One example was the international peace camp in Beilen, Drenthe, the Netherlands, in 1980. Annelies was part of the organization. On this camping area there were two thousand people from many different countries. During these two weeks, nonviolent actions were planned to be held at places that had associations with violence. A few examples were the NATO base in Havelterberg, the Johannes Postkazerne in Havelte and Holland Signaal in Enschede, where they make infrared binoculars for the army. There were trainings for demonstrations every day followed by a democratic camp meeting at which the plans for the next day were discussed, very typical of the seventies and eighties.

Harky, "I remember negotiating with the police, local inhabitants and participants about skinny dipping in the river by the camp. A funny moment occurred when a policeman asked me about the lady with the gray hair. I didn't immediately know who he meant. It appeared he was referring to my wife. I had not noticed her gray hair."

As on all vacations, the canoe came along, too. Douwe and a friend, both seven years old, discovered a very special use for the canoe. The boys earned money by renting out the canoe as a beer cooler.

Zeist

In 1989 the family moved to Zeist. This is a large town in the middle of the Netherlands close to Utrecht. Thea Lucia was already rooming in Zwolle, but came to Zeist later. The change was not simple for Douwe and Lena-Lynn, moving from a small rural village in Drenthe to a rather elite town in the middle of the Netherlands. Harky says, "Things did not go well for Douwe when we took Lena-Lynn along on vacation and he stayed home because he had just gotten a job. His friends took advantage of him, and he found it difficult to say no to them." The next summer Harky's in-laws came over, and both parents could go away with their minds at ease. His grandparent's presence made it possible for Douwe to say no to these friends, saying he had to take care of his grandparents. Douwe much respected the wisdom of his grandpa and was happy with the loving care of grandma. Douwe was saved from his 'friends' over several other summers because he went camping on vacation with the family of his best friend in Noord-Brabant, a province close to Belgium.

Douwe Harcourt (1973)

Douwe Harcourt (1973)

Douwe says, "My youth was good and safe. Yes, we were somewhat misfits with my eccentric father who made all kinds of inventions and had a strong accent, but we were part of the safe community of the village. There were always people in our house. We did a lot of things: picnics, swimming, and of course, barbecuing. We went canoeing on the little rivers in Drenthe. When we moved to Zeist, we went to the Henschotermeer, a little lake close by. I was sixteen at the time and didn't like it at all. Lena-Lynn, who was nine, loved it.

My father was always busy, was away from home a lot and lived somewhat in his own world. When he came home, he was often tired. Making reports and writing sermons caused him tension. My father gave us much freedom and my mother made the rules. I remember that they often quarreled. During vacations they were much nicer to each other. When I was about twelve, I didn't want to go to church anymore. Harky let me stay home. My parents were not legalistic; it was all about love.

Strangers always received a lot of attention. I sometimes thought: 'When is it my turn?' I think that I, more than my peers, learned that all people are equally valuable despite color of skin or whatever. If I had a fight, I was not always happy with my father's approach. He tried to work on my feelings, but I thought that you don't always have to accept everything and that desperate times require drastic measures. Later I saw that operating more tactically made more sense because no one benefits if a conflict escalates."

"When I was thirty-five and my father seventy, we went to the USA together. Then his background became clearer to me, and we became much closer. I see my parents often. They are always ready to help with the grandchildren. My daughter held a speech over Martin Luther King–her own idea–and my dad gladly came to school to hear it."

"Harky is always busy. I get tired just hearing his stories. Would I have made the same decisions in Harky's place? That is hard to say. I do not have the same open-mindedness and the same faith. But I do not judge my father. His choices were sometimes stressful for us, but we also had many good experiences. If I had grown up in a different family, I might not be working with victims of human trafficking. This work really suits me."

Friend of the family: Albert Mulder

When Douwe lived in Wilhelminaoord, he became friends with a teenage neighbor boy, Albert. Albert was seventeen when he first met Harky. The Klinefelters lived across the street from him in Wilhelminaoord and mostly had contact with Albert's parents. When Douwe was a teenager, he went to Albert and his ex-wife for advice.

When Harky and Annelies moved to Steenwijkerwold, Harky and this friend became real soul-mates. Albert is twelve years younger, but the difference in age makes no difference to their friendship.

The first time Harky and Albert did something together was when there was some ice. Harky came to Albert and asked if he could come along when Albert went ice skating. Albert remembers that it took Harky a long time to put on his skates. Albert had already skated around the Spokeplas, a large pond, twice before Harky was ready. It appeared that Harky couldn't skate at all! But he wanted to learn, so he took skating lessons. When Harky became the minister in Zeist, the two families spent part of their summer vacation together. The vicarage had enough room for guests. They did more things together. Visiting Avifauna, the bird park, was the beginning of bird watching together. That was their summer activity. In the winter they made skating trips.

After the period in Zeist, the Klinefelters came back up north and moved to Steenwijkerwold. From that time on, Albert and Harky visit each other every week. Albert joined peace demonstrations, thanks to the influence of the Klinefelters. He vividly remembers a meeting in Steenwijk, of WAAKS, where the atmosphere changed completely when Harky started talking. "The people turned around completely, really, all of them. I have never seen anything like it. He caught their attention without raising his voice." Albert remembers the first time he heard Harky deliver a speech, on a stage in The Hague. He had never seen him this inspired. His speech came right from his heart.

Harky wants to make use of every minute of his life. If the family is on its way to a lecture, there is just time to stop in at the store for something he needs. But if the girl at the cash register is taking a long time with a client before Harky, there is a problem. Albert has learned to accept Harky's continually late arrivals. But he says, "If I want him as a friend, I have to take him as he is."

Albert himself does not understand or speak English, but the deficient Dutch that Harky speaks is no problem for him. "I can understand him just fine."

Harky is very handy. Albert says, "For example, he is always working on the canoe. He keeps finding something new for it: a motor, a rudder."

Yes, they are different from each other. Harky likes to sit in an observation lookout; Albert likes to look while walking. Harky likes big birds, Albert likes small ones. Albert is always on time. Harky is always late.

Albert admires Harky. "What makes him so nice: he is completely genuine. He doesn't pretend; he really loves everyone. He doesn't have to exert himself in acts of nonviolence.

He never slips out of his role; he plays no role. Harky has had a great influence upon me. I have changed through him. I am a peace activist, just like him. Harky has taught me much about philosophy, for example. He is very good at explaining something. He really makes you think by making your thoughts wobble. He gave an example about a brilliant doctor who saved many lives, but also attacked a young girl. How do you judge someone like that? I don't think in black and white anymore. To Harky it is much more important to follow Jesus than to have a good knowledge of the Bible. I know Harky would rather have me be a believer, but he would rather see a good person who does not believe than a person of faith who does wrong."

Harky skating in Giethoorn, the Netherlands,

Isolated?

Were the children isolated because of the choices that their parents made? Probably some, Harky thinks, but he and Annelies also had good friends who were active for peace. They had children of the same age with whom their children could play. Through all kinds of other activities, they still were able to be part of the local community. When Harky and Annelies lived in Wilhelminaoord (1975 to 1989), they attended the Dutch Reformed Church, the village protestant church, simply to belong to the community, and also because that church had ecumenical tendencies. Later, when the children were older, they more often went to the Mennonite Church in Steenwijk.

Harky thinks the people probably found them a bit eccentric, but because of their openness and helpfulness they stayed in their good books. "Sometimes we were ahead of our times, but forerunners are needed to get the mass moving."

Annelies talks about Harky as father and pedagogue

"Harky was very easy going. He believed in a liberal upbringing. I didn't share his ideas at all. My limits were reached much sooner. That resulted in quarrels, and I know the children were not always happy with the situation. It made for uncertainty. Later we talked about it often, and now we think we would have done things differently. During the time in Wilhelminaoord, we were very busy and did not have much time for each other. That doesn't make it easy to talk things out or to consult each other.

Harky had nothing against alcohol or weed, while I found that you can't use those things in public with growing children. Not that Harky drank or smoked weed, but 'friends' did. My concern was setting a good example."

"In 1986 I was able to go to Assisi, Italy, for two weeks. Harky would take care of the family tasks. When I returned home earlier than expected, the house was a mess. I went away and said I would return in three hours. I expected the house to be cleaned up and supper ready. According to the children, they all worked very hard at it. When I came home everything was ship-shape. I know taking care of the children by himself asked much of Harky. Staying concentrated and keeping a regular schedule with them was not his thing. Getting the children to bed on time, getting them to the gym. Our children had to fend for themselves quite early. Harky still says: 'I thought I had another hour.'

Harky was not the type to go fishing with his children, but if a fishing rod had to be made or fixed, he was right there. Investigating something thoroughly and trying things out, and perfectionism and creativity are things the children learned from Harky. He had always invited the whole world into the house, and that helped form the children. They are not easily upset by 'strange people or other cultures.' We often had foreign guests of all kinds, like black people from Africa with their colorful robes and Indian people with white clothes and turbans. In our little Drenthe village, our guests were often an interesting attraction.

During the period of many guests, we often spoke English at home. This was good for the children. They all speak good English now. The children have also become critical thinkers who do their own thing, thanks to Harky."

When Harky no longer worked for the church in Zeist, he and Annelies moved from a house to an apartment building. He worked as a volunteer in a refugee center. He gathered discarded old bikes around the area and set up a bike repair shop in the refugee center. This led to pastoral connections. One of these contacts resulted the following event: in the refugee center was a young teenage girl who had become pregnant when she fled to the Netherlands. The refugee center called. They said that she wanted to give her baby up for adoption right away, but this could cause quite a commotion in the refugee center. Maybe, could she . . . Of course she could. On the day that the girl arrived at our home, she delivered the same night. It went smoothly. Daughter Lena-Lynn kept the baby warm until the midwife could take mother and child to the hospital for the formalities in the morning.

Lena-Lynn(1979)

Lena-Lynn (1979)

Lena-Lynn says, "I have had a good youth. Both parents were there to support us. I was left quite free, but there were boundaries. We discussed the rules; my parents were always ready to hear our arguments. Parents of children our age were often quite strict. I thought I had super parents. I know Thea Lucia has a completely different image of her childhood, but I was so much younger. I was ten when she moved out of the house.

My mother worked out. My father was a minister and often worked at home. I had to make my own sandwiches at an early age. My father is a night owl and has difficulty getting up early. My parents sometimes communicate rather abruptly with each other. That is simply their style. As a child I once asked them if they would ever separate because I had heard about fighting and divorces around me. We could talk about those kinds of things openly.

I loved canoeing with my father. He had made a construction to allow us to take a folding bike and trailer along in the canoe. We paddled along the Kromme Rijn River; afterwards, my father put the bike together, the canoe went onto the folding trailer, and we biked home. The barbecues at the Henschotermeer Lake are wonderful memories, too. My mother came directly to the lake from her work. My brother was older and didn't come along.

My father's special background was not talked about much. I know that during one history lesson about America, I said that my dad had worked together with Dr. Martin Luther King, Jr. The teacher said: 'Yes, and I played chess with God.' I didn't know much about the work he did.

There was concern when Harky went to Yugoslavia, but I trusted that he would come home safely. Giving trainings is really his calling, being a minister less so. Making sermons gives tension. There were constant worries about whether the congregation would understand Harky's Dutch. After the war in ex-Yugoslavia we went there on vacation. I found it very different. Some houses were demolished, others not. Squealers had reported where the 'wrong' people lived, and I could not imagine if some group went and murdered all Friesians in the Netherlands. Weird.

I have respect and admiration for my father. Conversations about what really matters formed us. I teach my own children that even one person can make a difference if there is bullying going on. I find it good to see that they choose to give the money they earned at the flea market to a good cause."

Inclusive loving attitude

During a service in the Mennonite Church of Steenwijk in October of 2013, Harky told those assembled about a special spiritual experience he had which binds him to his oldest daughter. Thea Lucia, who is a Shamanistic therapist, invited him to a ceremony in the Veluwe, a nature region in the middle of the Netherlands. After much deliberation Harky decided to go. He thought God wanted him to go, also to improve his relationship with his daughter. Harky has to admit that he had had little attention for her. The rituals moved him, and also his daughter's words. She had prayed that he would come. He experienced God's presence.

Through this open attitude, Harky can always reach the heart of his children.

Another example is Harky's contribution to the wedding ceremony of Thea Lucia and Ronald in 2008. Thea Lucia had been studying Shamanism for some time. For her wedding service, Harky combined elements of Native American rituals and the wedding service of the Church of England. Harky has precious memories of this very personal ceremony with enthusiastic and radiant children and beautiful fall weather in a lovely natural setting.

During the wedding of his son Douwe(now divorced) Harky read parts from the Libanees writer Kahil Gibran's book "The Prophet". Also some African symbolisms were part as the bride grew up in Burkina Faso.

Harky was also involved in his other daughter's wedding. For Lena-Lynn and Jeroen's ceremony, Harky wrote a personal blessing, combining it with memories of a joint trip to the US and Canada.

> May your love be as great as the Rocky Mountains
> As high as the Empire State Building
> As deep as the Atlantic Ocean
> As warm as the hot springs of Fairmont
> As powerful as the glaciers of the Ice Fields
> As exciting as rafting on the rapids of the Columbia River
> As safe as an osprey's nest
> As strong as the black bears
> As tender as the deer
> As permanent as the stars.

Raising Courageous Citizens

An anonymous poem does a good job of putting Harky and Annelies' ideas about their love into words:

LOVE

I love you,
Not only for what you are,
But for what am
When I am with you.
I love you,
Not only for what
You have made of yourself,
But for what
You are making of me.
I love you,
For the part of me
That you bring out;
I love you
For putting your hand
Into my heaped-up heart
And passing over
All the foolish, weak things
That you can't help
Dimly seeing there,
And for drawing out
Into the light
All the beautiful belongings
That no one else had looked
Quite far enough to find.
I love you because you
Are helping me to make
Not a tavern
But a temple;
Out of the works
Of my every day
Not a reproach
But a song . . .

Anonymous

Christmas card with wedding photo Harky and Annelies, Drachten, the Netherlands, 1966

On December 29 2006, Harky and Annelies had a special 40th Anniversary celebration. At that time, Harky, looking back upon their forty years of marriage, said, "In our lives Annelies and I were inspired by Dr. Martin Luther King whom we both knew personally. Based on this inspiration, our goal has been to work with movements for peace and justice. Our belief in the love of God, as Jesus of Nazareth has shown it, is the ground of our hope for the future and our growing capacity to give love, not only to each other, our family and friends, but also to the rejected and even to enemies. Faith is not a burden but a source of power and even more of joy."

Annelies writes about her marriage with Harky, "When I married Harky, I knew that I was marrying someone who had a big heart for the whole world, and that I would never have him for myself alone. There are always surprises and challenges since he responds whenever a serious peace and justice issue arises. Never a dull moment with Harky! Peace and justice are his passion and his motivation in life, and he puts all his intelligence and courage toward them. He needs inspiration and space. He has his own pace and priorities. The most beautiful aspects of being married to Harky are his unconditional love, dependability, patience, and creativity."

Working together towards peace and justice

In the past, Harky and Annelies both had their own fields of work. Harky was mostly concerned with trainings in nonviolence within the Netherlands and in the rest of the world. Annelies started the project called Nonviolent Society through the Mennonite Community. She was the coordinator of this mediation project for church and society for ten years. She co-authored the Dutch book *Mediation in het Pastoraat* which has also been translated into English as *Mediation in Pastoral Care*. She was a board member of the IFOR (International Fellowship of Reconciliation) for many years. Presently Annelies is chairwomen of CPT Netherlands and board member of CPT International.

Harky about Annelies

Harky readily says, "Without Annelies I would not have been able to do what I have done. We both did our own thing in our lives, but we share the desire to work towards a better world. I am very thankful for this. Even during the times I took dangerous risks, Annelies always supported me, and I realize that it sometimes must have been very tense for her. When I was a hippie-pastor, she was afraid they might find drugs in our house, brought in by one of the many guests. Then she feared that I would be arrested, Annelies sent back to the Netherlands, and Thea Lucia placed in an institution. It was also very tense for her when I offered to take the place of a hostage during the train kidnapping.

Annelies can do many things at the same time. I admire how she can combine her work on the boards of diverse organizations and in the church and combine this with the care she gives to the children and the people in our neighborhood. She can listen much better than I can. She makes sure that my sermons, lectures, and articles are set into understandable Dutch. We supplement each other.

A poet once said that a pine tree and an oak tree stand beside each other but not in each other's shadow. That's how it is with us. We give each other space to do what we find important. It makes me very happy that I can completely trust Annelies."

Fatherhood

In retrospect it is possible to question some of the choices Harky made, but at the moment itself, the choices all seemed very natural.

No, of course he never considered not continuing life with Annelies: he is much too much in love! And, like most couples, they wanted children. They were even checking into the possibility of adoption because they thought Harky might be less fertile because of his illnesses during his teens. They decided that Annelies should stop taking the pill and wait and see. Just when Harky had lost his job with SCLC, Annelies became pregnant. They were very happy!

Harky says that his own father was not a good example of how to be an involved parent. Harky realized that he should have done more with his own children, especially when Douwe once came home all excited after one of the Malukans had taken him to the circus. He had had the time of his life! Then Harky realized he should do this kind of thing with his children and not merely follow in his father's footsteps. He had flashes of the need his children had for him several times. Once during a training session in the Adult Education Center, he envisioned Douwe sitting there. He needed him and wanted to climb onto his lap.

In another dream he saw Thea Lucia in danger: she sat in a car that had hit water.

If Harky had courses at the Center which took several days, Annelies always took the children for at least one meal with him there. Early on, he would come home from a course in the Adult Center so emotionally drained that he could pay no attention at all to the children. Not surprisingly, this usually happened at supper time, the most challenging time of the day for a family. He solved the problem this way: instead of going directly home he spent a few hours alone to come to himself so he could give the children attention. He learned that it is better to delay something than to do it halfway. This was a win-win solution for all parties: Harky came home rested and could give attention to his wife and children, and everybody was happy.

A constant for the family was that sometimes Harky took great risks when he became involved in solving conflicts worldwide. Annelies fully supported him, and Harky trusted that all would turn out well for the children if he did not come home alive. He points to the Bible passage where Jesus says that whoever will follow him must find Jesus more important than his family. In this, Dr. Martin Luther King, who did his work realizing that his children might unexpectedly lose their father at an early age, was his example.

Harky realized you need other people to help you raise your children. As he stated, his own father had not been a good role model. The father of Annelies (Heit) became an excellent model. From the first day they met they felt soul brothers and there was a great respect toward each other. Heit helped Harky , in a very quiet way, to become a better father by showing him how his actions or non-actions had impact on the children and Annelies. His own family in the United States, a sister, was too far away to be a sounding board.

Harky feels grateful for the support he has had during his life from his Dutch family.

Lena, sister of Annelies

Lena is the younger sister of Annelies. Harky is thankful for the cordial relationship he has with his sister- and brother-in law. Lena tells, "Annelies and I are five years apart. When you are young, that is a large gap. We didn't do much together then. In 1965 Annelies (19 years old) went to America for a year. I was quite proud of my sister. I remember that my parents found it rather tense, but they were also proud that this possibility existed for their daughter."

"When the year was nearly over, Annelies told us she had fallen in love with an American and wanted to marry him, but she was only twenty and needed her parents' consent to marry. My father was quite clear, "If he really loves you, he'll come get you!" So, Annelies came home alone.

A few months later (December of 1966), Harky followed. We picked him up at the station in Heerenveen. He greeted us with the following greeting, with a heavy American accent, "Nice to meet you." I liked Harky right away and thought he cared greatly for Annelies to come all the way to the Netherlands to marry her. They married at the end of December and left for America in February. The next year our contact consisted of letter writing and a few telephone calls. In 1970 Annelies came over for a few weeks with Thea Lucia."

Brother-in-law Ben (husband of Lena), "My first real contact with Harky and Annelies was in 1971. Lena and I spent a month visiting them in America. What I noticed first was the ease with which they shared everything with everybody. Material things did not interest them much. I think of Harky as a courageous man, not in the sense of being tough, but of being courageous in his convictions. He dares undertake actions that can involve risks. One example is that he was prepared to take the place of a hijack victim during the hijacking of the train at De Punt."

"If Harky finds something important he really goes to work. I remember that he once wanted to buy a new guitar. This was very important to him, because playing guitar is his passion. We roamed through all of Rotterdam (where I lived then) and visited all the music stores. He took his time, playing the guitars and talking to the sales people. The nice thing about this is, that, when he finally makes a choice, even years later, it still seems to have been the right one."

"In 1972 Harky and Annelies moved to the Netherlands. Their first period was difficult for both of them. I tried to help as much as possible during this time, and it went further than helping them move, paint, and decorate the house. I tried to help them find their way in the Netherlands and try to build a future. Especially during the time that Harky was jobless and during some difficult times in Zeist, we had very regular and deep discussions. It is easy to understand that it was difficult for Harky to accept that he was forced to do factory work, different from anything he had done in America. We talked about that too.

The children made our contact even more intens. If Harky and Annelies needed to go to America (for example, for a funeral), one telephone call was enough. An hour later, Thea Lucia was with us and they could go their way. Later, when the children were older, I had the chance to help with their growing up. It was clear that the emotional charge was high in such cases. Later, when our parents' health declined, we had intensive discussions as to how we could handle this responsibility the best, despite our different convictions.

Besides all this we had the usual family gatherings: birthdays, New Year's Eve, getting together in Eernewoude where our parents had a trailer for camping. We did boating, skating in Giethoorn and surroundings, sleepovers of the children. Helping vulnerable people binds us, although we each do it in our own manner. For Harky and Annelies it is their commitment for life, we do it simply as our responsibility to society."

Yale time friends Paul and Sally Harris

As it turned out, deep friendships did not come only from the Netherlands. Very good friends from the time Harky was at Yale University Theological Seminary (1967) have stayed next to him and his whole family.

Paul and Sally Harris, St. Paul, Minnesota, 2016

Harky, "When I picked up my studies again, Annelies and I stayed in the married students' dormitory. There we learned to know Paul and Sally Harris."

Paul writes, "Our friendship with Harky and Annelies has been a strange, intermittent and powerfully blessed one. Harky was in his concluding year and I in my first year. It didn't take long for our friendship to flourish and take both roots and wings. Soon there were shared meals, shared meetings with various groups we were involved in, and shared sorrows, the most significant being the death of Dr. Martin Luther King, Jr. in 1968.

There are many kinds of relationships. Ours has been of the kind that, even with a lacunae of many years, picked right up where we left off. After Harky graduated, we didn't hear from Harky and Annelies for over a year when, out of the blue, we were invited to come to New Jersey for Harky's ordination. Another chunk of time passed before a letter with a Dutch stamp told us of their move to the Netherlands. More time passed, and we heard that they were going to visit us at our rustic cabin in Michigan's Upper Peninsula. Harky said he had a gift for me. The noun should have been plural since the gift was boxes and boxes of books. Suddenly we had a big theological library."

Years slipped by and children were born. In the early '80s, Paul attended a conference in Strasbourg. While Paul spent a week there, Sally and their son, Ken, went to visit the Klinefelters' in Friesland, the northwest province of the Netherlands. Sally and Annelies both felt the relationship had gone right back to the loving, supportive relationship of their time together in the early 1970's. But then something strange happened. Both Klinefelters' and Harris's letters were regularly returned to their senders. Paul wrote Yale Divinity School for the Klinefelters' address. Harky wrote Yale for the Harris's address. Nothing worked for a period of about twenty years.

About ten years ago, the Harris's telephone rang, and an unforgettable voice could be heard asking for Paul Harris. Harky had been to a Yale reunion and had found Paul's telephone number.

Paul and Sally, doing annual short-term mission stints in Tanzania for the Evangelical Church in America (ELCA), were flying through Amsterdam twice a year on their way to and from Tanzania. It occurred to Harky that the Harrises could book lay-overs on the way back to the US. The Klinefelters invited them to stop and visit them.

Getting off their plane at Schiphol in 2011, Paul and Sally were on the lookout for their long-sundered friends. The Harrises wondered, "Would we recognize each other? What would connect us after almost twenty five years of separation? Would the passion for social justice still be burning brightly? A silver-haired woman came up, scanning the crowd of waiting people. Could this be Annelies? There had been no silver hair the last time. However, there was the same strong, confident countenance and the purposeful stride. Behind her an older guy, also gray-haired, followed with the iconic "Harky shuffle." It was indeed them, and we were all together again. The train trip to Steenwijkerwold took about two hours. Before it was over, the stories of our families, work and lives had been well rehearsed. There had been many triumphs and some very rough patches in life, family and work. But our core identities linked with faith in God, love of family, and determination to make our work help the world be a more peaceful, just place were unshaken and undiminished."

The stop-over at Schiphol became a yearly event. During our annual sojourns in Africa, we had developed a love of bird watching. We had also developed a common delight in cross-country skiing, camping and canoeing. We were proud of our children and adored our grandchildren.

"The Klinefelters are best described as 'flourishing.' They are alive and enlivening. They are guardians of the heritage of Dr. Martin Luther King, Jr. and keep King's legacy alive and flourishing throughout the world. They are alive to the wonders of God's creation and are powerfully active in doing God's work in this broken and breaking world. They know how to unsolicitly encourage and affirm their friends, neighbors and family.

We look at the lives that Annelies and Harky continue to live and are blessed by the energy and vision, love and compassion, interest and knowledge their lives radiate to all who are fortunate to be caught up in the life of these amazing people."

The present family

The oldest daughter, Thea Lucia, is married to Ronald. She is a Shamanic therapist and gives workshops and does coaching. Douwe is divorced, has joint custody of his daughter, has a new girlfriend Nadia and works with juvenile traumatized refugees. Lena-Lynn is married to Jeroen and has two children. She has a daycare center in her house.

During their family get-togethers, Harky has all the time in the world for his grandchildren.

He has something special with each of them: with Luca it is horses and guitar playing, with Eline there is a joint interest in the universem, creativity and skating, with Martijn he shares a compassion for adventure and doing things with your hands. What Harky likes most is to go away with them in the camper. They camp out, go canoeing, enjoy nature and bird-watching, playing guitar, and eating ice cream. Harky also gladly goes along to school to give a practical lesson on nonviolent self-defense in the context of a speech about Dr. King by his granddaughters. A friend of one of his granddaughters held a speech on Dr. King and asked Harky to come give a lesson on nonviolent actions. Through his open attitude, Harky can always reach the heart of his children and grandchildren.

During the years, Harky has discovered that you remain father and child-raiser your whole life long, just as being a minister is a life-long task. Pastoral and nonviolent skills (such as nonviolent communication and mediation) always come in handy. You need a solid home base and a deeply rooted mental power to be able to carry on. And yet, you always have to compromise between being a father and a peace apostle, between being away and taking a breather, between choosing for yourself and giving all the room to the other.

Harky, "If someone asks me: 'How do you keep up this life and work?' I say: 'If you have the privilege of having a family and friends who are forgiving and let you be who you are with all your passions and qualities, then you are rich and can take on the world.'"

This chapter has been about Harky's ideals, which sometimes clashed with each other: that of father and peace apostle. The children are now grown, but Harky finds that his dilemma has not gone away. When he was raising children, their interests and needs sometimes clashed with his peace work. Now, in his eighties, he still feels the same dilemma, deepened by the pressure of time. Confronted with all the needs of people he calls neighbors, Harky feels torn apart. He expressed this in a sermon in October 2013. "In the fall of my life, I become more confronted than ever with the dilemma of how I should spend the short time that is left to me: passing on my spiritual ideals to generations after me, or in giving personal attention to the neighbor who can knock on my door at any moment."

Harky and Annelies, Steenwijkerwold, the Netherlands, 2014

—9—

You Can Kill the Dreamer, but Not the Dream

"The real core of true nonviolence is the belief that every person is an indispensable part of the cosmos and that the greatest power in the universe is love."

—Harcourt Klinefelter

Even in his elderly years, Harky is still the scout who learned that you should always leave a campsite in better condition than you found it. For example, you should leave more kindling wood than was available when you came. That is what Harky wants to do with the world, his campsite. He tries to use the talents and possibilities he is offered to benefit all of mankind. He says, "I have witnessed with my own eyes how great the power of nonviolence is. That is why I am convinced that, not the way of the sword, but the way of nonviolence is the way to achieve justice and long-lasting peace. With the way of the sword, the goal is to frighten people and rule over them; everything is aimed at guaranteeing one's own safety. The way of nonviolence has opposite goals. There the goal is to banish fear with love and offer everyone a life of peace and hope."

Dr. Martin Luther King has shown Harky this way of love.

Pragmatist

Harky loves to philosophize, but being practical is more important. As a pragmatist, he chooses what will work. When Gandhi was asked how you learn nonviolence, he answered, "You do not teach nonviolence, you do it." Harky can say the same.

Being practical is the directive that gives shape to theory = inductive learning from practice to theory. This was evident in the very first sermon Harky delivered in America. He used the example of a skeptical young boy who was not convinced by the arguments he heard during discussions in the youth group, but who was convinced through the behavior of the young people who lived the Bible.

Interrelated Problems

Dr. King believed in the interrelation between racial discrimination, poverty and militarism (war). After his death, another factor was added: environment (preservation of creation). Harky is still active on all of these fronts.

A–Racism–discrimination

Harky says, "We are all discriminated against and we all discriminate." He is very involved in the battle against those who knowingly discriminate (for example, some political leaders) and the task of helping people become aware of their own unconscious discrimination. Harky notes, "Unconscious discrimination determines our decisions and our behavior. It is important to become aware of this. Only if people are convinced that all people are equal can a fundamental change be realized. As long as we regard people as Jewish or heathen, Catholic or Protestant, Chinese or American, black or white, man or women, LBTGQ, we will never succeed in seeing them as fellow human beings made of the same material as we are.

The worst kind of racism is the apartheid and segregation set down by law. Each in his own land, Gandhi and King have both made an end to this detestable form of discrimination based on the color of skin. As president, Nelson Mandela in South Africa has tried to build a just society by organizing meetings of reconciliation where parties tried to reach out to each other by admitting guilt and pronouncing forgiveness."

Actual examples

In October of 2017, Harky and Annelies made a special trip. They went to America and visited the places where Dr. Martin Luther King had made a difference. A group of television program makers accompanied them to hear the stories of the people and learn about the encounters they had had a half-century ago. Everything was filmed for a Dutch television documentary to commemorate the assassination of Martin Luther King on April 4, 1968.

About that trip, Harky recounts, "We entered a (formerly all black) café in Selma and I realized that we could not have done so fifty years ago. If we had, we would probably have been killed by white racists, just as Rev. Reeb was."

The protests of the *Black Lives Matter* movement sound exactly like the Civil Rights Movement of that era. It appears that the life of a black is still worth less than that of a white.

Harky approves of discussions like the one in the Netherlands about the black assistant (*Zwarte Piet*) to Saint Nicholas because they help raise awareness of unconscious discrimination. *Black Lives Matter* in the US and comparable movements in the Netherlands contribute to making sure that police violence (sometimes based on open discrimination, sometimes unconscious) gets publicity and that measures are taken to stop discrimination. In the Netherlands there is now a special training for police to remove the taboos about discussing the subjects of racism and sexism so that the police can help each other to deal with such issues as professionals.

It is important to Harky that the concerns of those who identify as LHBTQ (lesbian, homo, bisexual, trans-gender, and queers) are now discussed more openly and that the *#Me Too* movement justifiably asks for society's attention to deeply-rooted sexism. He says, "Fortunately, at an intellectual level, we have accepted that our sexual inclination is inherited, not learned. Before change can occur at the emotional level, however, we first have to change our convictions. As long as people say that they do not discriminate, they are like alcoholics who say, 'I have no drinking problem.'"

Racism also plays an important role in helping refugees. Refugees from Africa are, on the whole, more often turned away than people from other parts of the world. This has to do with skin color and with other cultural and social backgrounds. Many people simply assume that Africans will not fit in anyway.

Dr. Martin Luther King said it is our moral obligation to work with unwavering determination on exterminating discrimination globally. According to King, discrimination is not only an American phenomenon. If Western civilization does not react constructively to the challenge of banning discrimination, Dr. King predicts that future historians will say that a great civilization was lost because they did not have the courage to fight for justice for all of their citizens with all their heart.

B–Poverty

Technical revolutions cause social problems. In 1966, long before there were computers, Dr. King foresaw a time when the government would probably need to finance massive job opportunity projects because there would be no more requests for manual labor. In the Poor Peoples Campaign of 1968 he pleaded for a Basic Annual Wage for everyone. Currently, there are experiments of this nature in Wageningen, the Netherlands, and Canada

Yes, now you can, as a white person, enter a black café without problems, but in your hotel you will probably not see blacks except as personnel. The issue of blacks being limited to low-paying jobs that keep them in poverty is still not adequately addressed. And, of course, poverty is connected to the social problems of discrimination, dilapidation, violence, educational disadvantage, unemployment, violence between citizens and police, possession of weapons, drug use, crime. On his trips through the USA, Harky is shocked at the increase in poverty he saw in some of the places he had been fifty years before.

Poverty can also be the result of land expropriation as in Columbia, where Christian Peacemaker Teams (CPT) keep an eye on the situation and publish to the world at large what is going on. In a time in which products are flown all over the world, in the Netherlands people can protest against certain multinationals by boycotting their products. In this way one can force these multinationals to stop confiscating land in Columbia. The goal is to take responsibility here at home to help fight poverty elsewhere.

C–Militarism-terrorism and nonviolence

After a lecture at the University of Utrecht, the Netherlands (*Hogeschool Utrecht*) in December 2016, Harky received the following question: Do you think that nonviolence would work in Syria? He responded, "Yes, definitely.

All great religions say that you should not inflict others with actions that you would not like to receive yourself. Jesus went further and said: 'Do unto others as you would have them do unto you.' Jesus formulates it in a positive way."

At a personal level, we give presents to our children and friends, often without really expecting anything in return. But what about at the social level? Can this principle work there too? Governmental foreign aid work comes close, but often only happens because of an economic relationship between countries. It would be better to meet the need for foreign aid with love and from a sense of justice. The Bible directly addresses this issue. Proverbs 25.21 says, "If your enemy is hungry, feed him, and if he is thirsty give him something to drink." Repeating this statement in his letter to the Romans, St. Paul adds, "Do not be overcome by evil, but overcome evil with good." (Romans 12.21)

Harky asks, "What would happen if we used a fraction of the money we invest in fighter planes to build a field hospital in Syria? Use your imagination! The whole situation would be different. If we would invest in nonviolent observers and helpers, we could create a world for our children which is much different than the world in which we live. I think that change is possible. You have to use your imagination in a radical manner. And I hope that there are people who will use their intelligence and ask themselves what would happen if they took this advice to heart."

At the time in September of 2017 when the US and North Korea threatened each other with a nuclear war, it was made public that South Korea had decided to send food, medicine and other goods to North Korea. According to Harky, this is proof that his ideas are not so crazy after all.

Armament

Harky spent many years protesting against nuclear arms and is very happy that the 2017 Nobel Peace Prize went to the *International Campaign to Abolish Nuclear Weapons* (ICAN). This organization calls upon governments to work on an agreement that will lead to worldwide abolition of nuclear arms. How laborious this progress is, however, is shown by the fact that the Netherlands has not yet signed this treaty.

Refugees and the weapon industry

People have always fled both war and economic disaster. Now many people are fleeing the disastrous effects of climate change which are mostly caused by the way we treat the environment.

Instead of helping solve the problems refugees are facing, preventing refugees from crossing the Mediterranean Sea has become militarized. Coast Guard and Frontex ships are equipped as military vessels, even though they are no part of the marines. (Frontex is a European agency which helps member countries to control borders.) This is a new source of income for the weapons industry. The militarization of these services keeps demanding Harky's attention and, as a press agent, he tries to publish information about these activities widely in the hope of provoking a social debate.

A news article on refugees gave Harky a short-lived hope. Dr. King believed that unearned suffering has a redeeming power. No matter how great the evil is, the power of love is even stronger. Sometimes this becomes evident completely unexpectedly. In 2015 there was a picture in the news showing a dead child on a beach. A day later the Dutch newspaper *Trouw* placed a picture on the front page of a stream of people walking along the highway with the headline, "Exodus out of Hungary." The accompanying article said, "The pictures of thousands of refugees walking along the highway to Vienna reminds one of an exodus of biblical portions. A few Samaritans stood along the emergency lane with bottles of water or stuffed toys." Suddenly the news about refugees was placed in a more positive light. Harky hoped this signaled a new perspective on refugees.

Sadly, we in Europe closed the borders shortly after this.

Overcoming post traumatic stress

A war causes many victims and many traumatic experiences. Fortunately methods have been developed to help people learn to live with these stress factors. Harky has helped people learn to be stress workers. During the *Mayday* demonstrations against the war in Vietnam in 1971, he became friends with Laura Hessler who later settled in the Netherlands. She founded *Musicians Without Borders*. This organization hopes that music and dance can help children and adults to overcome stress experiences in places, among others, like Palestine and the Congo. The teachers are often refugees themselves and understand the emotions of the participants.

Another friend of Harky's is Dr. Charles Tauber who became inspired by the work Harky did in former Yugoslavia. He has been working in Vukovar (Serbia) since the eighties, helping traumatized war veterans through the *Coalition for Work with Psycho trauma and Peace*.

D-Environment

During the years that Dr. King was alive, few people were concerned with environmental issues. After the report of the *Club of Rome* in 1972, more attention was paid to the environment. Harky was also affected by this subject. He was responsible for trainings as preparation of large demonstrations, such as the one in 1979 in which twenty-five thousand people demonstrated against storing nuclear material in the salt domes of Gasselte, the Netherlands and another in 1980 against the nuclear plant at Dodewaard, the Netherlands. It is a constant struggle between what is good for the earth and its people, and what is good for the economy. A recent example of this is the inherent dangers in natural gas extraction now evident in Groningen, a province in the north of the Netherlands. For decades gas has been extracted from the largest natural gas bell in Europe. It is a major source of income for the country. Recently, there have been a series of earthquakes and thousands of homes and hundred of churches have been damaged. They discovered that they were caused by the removal of the gas which caused the ground to sink. There have been many protests. Harky was involved as an advisor for an action group.

The Life of Peace Apostle Harcourt Klinefelter

Project van de North Atlantic DE-FENCE Movement
Reclaiming military ground for civil use
Terugwinning van militair terrein voor een civiele bestemming

▲ 'Harky', de Nederlands-Amerikaanse dominee, spreekt de 'bezetters' toe van achter een hek.

Action at the Johannes Post army base, Havelte, the Netherlands, 1988

An example of the relation between environment and war was an activity in which Harky was involved in 1988. On a Sunday morning, at ten o'clock, in a living room in Wilhelminaoord, Harky quoted the passage from Isaiah 2:4 about hammering swords into plowshares and spears into pruning hooks. Then the start signal was given for a demonstration at the Johannes Post Army Barracks in Havelte. Twelve men and women picked up their rakes, hoes, spades, tools and a plowshare. A mission awaited. Symbolically, they were going to work up the land that was being used for military purposes to make it suitable for farming." When the demonstrations were no longer necessary because there were no more rockets in Havelte, Harky helped with the founding of a fair trade store (fighting poverty) and a second-hand store (environment protection) in Steenwijk.

The camper and the environment

Harky recalls, "When Annelies's mother died, we bought a small, second-hand diesel camper with the inheritance money. At that time, diesel was seen as being less polluting than gasoline. It was also cheaper. By buying the camper, we hit two birds with one stone. We used it to go to peace conferences outside the Netherlands and combine the trips with vacations. Ironically enough, now diesel motors are regarded as being very polluting. Sometimes time catches up on your good intentions. "

Camper at the Peace Event, Sarajevo, Bosnia, 2014

Once a press agent, always a press agent

Dr. King said that the goal of demonstrations was to expose injustice and thereby activate the conscience of citizens. Those people could in turn exert pressure on the government to change the situation. Modern technology has made this easier to do. When Harky worked with Dr. King, he had a tape recorder. At the time this was something quite out of the ordinary. He used a land-line telephone to relate the news to the media about what Dr. King had said and done. Now, almost everyone has access making recordings via smart phones and disseminating them via social media. This means that recordings of protests on the one hand, or of police or other violence on the other hand can be spread all over the world instantaneously.

Tips from Harcourt Klinefelter to expose mistakes in thinking and deception

"Speak Truth to Power" is an old Quaker slogan which is very relevant now that we are confronted with fake news and alternative facts. Back in 2009, Harky published the following tips in a book about war propaganda and the manipulation of the news.

These four tips bear repeating here.

They are warnings to be on the alert for:

Words that qualify instead of giving pure facts

Words like *terrorists, criminals, innocent victims, retaliation actions,* and the like are qualifying words. Usually the people on 'our' side are seen and described as heroes and freedom fighters, and people on 'the other' side as cowards and terrorists.

You often see news reports like the following: 'terrorists' have 'killed' five 'innocent civilians' in an 'attack' and the 'army' was 'forced' to 'react' using a 'retaliation action; in which forty people 'perished.' It is clear: the enemy is the personification of evil and 'we' could only react. Not only is this often a misleading representation of situations, it takes attention away from the fact that, during retaliation activities, more people may die than during the action upon which one is reacting.

Try to report news using neutral words.

Classification mistakes in comparisons

We know that we cannot compare apples and pears, but when politics is concerned, it is not always that simple. We see that economic systems, regimes, and religions, all of these being separate categories, are often mixed together. We then see news about 'Muslim' terrorists and 'democratic' government troops: in cases like these, descriptors conflate religion and politics.

Try to call out such conflations.

Over-simplification of conflicts

Where conflicts are concerned, nuances are often lost. During the Cold War, many people in the West thought in terms of a dichotomy of democratic-capitalism-religion versus totalitarian-communist-atheism, or even simpler: freedom versus lack of freedom. That other combinations might be possible or even already exist was out of the question, and people did not perceive other variations such as a capitalistic dictatorship or democratic socialism. Also little attention was paid to the lack of freedom and injustice that capitalism (the 'free market economy') brought to many people.

Try not to oversimplify conflicts.

Disguised forms of censorship

Censorship is difficult to discover. How can you know what you are missing? Only if you have access to more sources. The best thing to do is to gather as much material as possible and compare. The free press is not as free as often thought. Who has access to the media? In the US, all political parties have the right to equal time on TV—if they can pay for it. In actuality, only two parties have access because of the cost. Internet offers many opportunities to get a better picture, but that only pertains to those who look for alternative reports and know how to look. Nevertheless, here lie chances for the peace movement.

Seek multiple sources that articulate multiple perspectives.

Influence

Harky realizes that he was in the right place at the right time several times. He calls it surfing on the waves of the civil rights movement and the peace movement. He was fortunate to be working in the Center in Havelte, where his talents to work for peace and justice were useful. Was it coincidence? He believes not, but will also never say it was predestined. To him, it is clear that there were too many opportunities crossing his path to say it was all merely coincidence.

Influence cannot be measured, but it is a clear fact that Harky is good at using the possibilities handed to him to tell his story. He is still approached by reporters of newspapers, magazines, radio and television. Harky is still very inspiring, even at his advanced age. But he is no Martin Luther King. How great is his influence actually?

Harky as trainer, Ireland, 2013

Annelies has the tendency to estimate Harky's influence to be greater than he does. She regularly meets people who say that Harky's actions and words have touched them and they have put his words in action. She calls him a man of integrity, interested, and charismatic—someone who makes an impression. She emphasizes that he has reached many people as a trainer, during his courses, as a minister in the congregation, through his work in refugee centers, in schools, and universities.

Refugee work seen through the eyes of a child

In 2016 Harky did a program on Dr. King at the school of child named Merlijn (10 years old), supplemented with exercises in nonviolence. Working with refugees on Lesbos was also mentioned.

He was pleasantly surprised on Sunday, December 17, 2017, when he saw a children's program on television (*Zapp Echt Gebeurd*). It showed a film about Merlijn (now 11 years old) playing with refugee children on Lesbos. His mother had spent time there as a nurse and thought it a good idea to have her son learn about the way of life of these refugees. It was an impressive story.

Carefully, but conscious of the role he played, Harky sometimes points to news facts which could be connected to the trainings in handling conflicts through a nonviolent approach which he gave during the war in the Balkan. The fact that there are now training centers in Serbia, Croatia, and Bosnia, which have trained hundreds of people in nonviolence as well as centers in almost 50 other countries shows that such training is significant.

Others talk about Harky's influence

Lynn Gibb

Harky's sister calls him, "very influential as an organizer, leader, speaker, minister, and simply as someone to talk to. He has accomplished changes and inspired many (young) people to serve and to work toward a better future."

Dr. Fernando Enns

Dr. Fernando Enns, professor of peace theology and ethics in the Free University/*Vrije Universiteit* in Amsterdam, calls Harky definitely influential, especially in the Mennonite world in the Netherlands. "But his influence goes farther. If you change the life of one person, you change the world. His unique story about Martin Luther King, which he tells with deep conviction, is very inspiring. People take nonviolence more seriously through this."

Dr. Fernando Enns has seen it in the master students whom Harky addressed at the beginning of the academic year. "He tells his story, and the fact itself that someone who was an eyewitness of the world changing events concerning Civil Rights in America in the sixties was fascinating and enriching for the group." According to professor Enns there are two manners of observation. "You can observe reality as it comes to you, and become disillusioned. But, you can also look with other eyes, God's eyes, as it were, and then you see signs everywhere of a partly achieved and still ongoing Kingdom of God. What we see is not the end of the story: love will overcome. Stepping outside the circle of violence is important because it connects with what God is doing.

Who could have imagined that the Berlin Wall would fall through only nonviolent power? Who had dared predict that the apartheid regime in South-Africa would come to an end without a civil war? We need courageous people who really believe that the dream of peace can become a reality and act accordingly. Harky is a shining example of this."

Daan Savert

Daan Savert, theologian and pacifist, describes Harky as follows, "According to me, Harky is an important bridge between old and young generations. He was press agent of Martin Luther King and can tell, better than anyone else, what it meant to be part of that movement in the sixties. Even more than this, he, at the age of 80, keeps asking himself what King's view on nonviolent struggle for justice would be in this day. Last year he and his wife Annelies went to Lesbos together to support the Christian Peacemaker Teams.

When I was involved with the CPT and took part in a delegation in Iraq-Kurdistan, it was an enormous encouragement to discover that a man with such experience and wisdom was also part of this organization. I am impressed with the deeply-rooted faith of Harky. When he sees crucifixions, he finds it time for a resurrection. While many people, including Christians, keep believing in the power of weapons and a strong army, Harky stays in the footsteps of King and hammers on the fact that violence is never the way. That is why Harky, in all his modesty, is a modern prophet who gets my heart as well as my hands moving."

You Can Kill the Dreamer, but Not the Dream

Marjolein Leusink

Marjolein Leusink, a student at the University of Utrecht, the Netherlands, wrote Harky after hearing his lecture at the school, "I would like to thank you for your inspiring words on December 9, 2016. I was very moved by all the things you told us and it has been on my mind all week considering the things that are going on in the world today. I feel honored to have met you and to hear about Martin Luther King's life from someone who actually worked with him. I loved hearing about your experiences and solutions to difficult situations and how the Bible inspired you to do so. I would like to thank you for participating in the Civil Rights Movement and for choosing to put yourself in danger for what is right. Were it not for people like you, these things might not have changed. Thank you for setting the example and showing the world how change can be obtained without using violence. I really appreciate it that people like you stood up and fought for what is right. I hope that I can be part of that one day. You are a true inspiration and I will never forget this afternoon at the University. I will try to teach my students the things you taught me so that no one will forget."

Final phase of life

Working as a man of peace sometimes means looking death in the eye.

According to Harky, fear of death is a survival mechanism. Except for this natural fear, Harky does not dread death. He hopes that he will be able to keep his wits about him until the end. He hopes to "die in the harness" that is to die on the job.

Harky has often stood face to face with death. When he was about 15 or 16, for months he lived with the thought that he had cancer and would die. Later he often took risks in the fight for equal rights for black and white and in other conflict situations. Life after death has no material form according to Harky. He would like to believe that people who have died live on in another dimension. "It is better to live with the idea that life goes on than with the idea that everything is over after death. Otherwise you spend your whole life merely trying to stay alive." Martin Luther King's vision that death is not a dead-end street, only a bend in the road we can't see through, appeals to him.

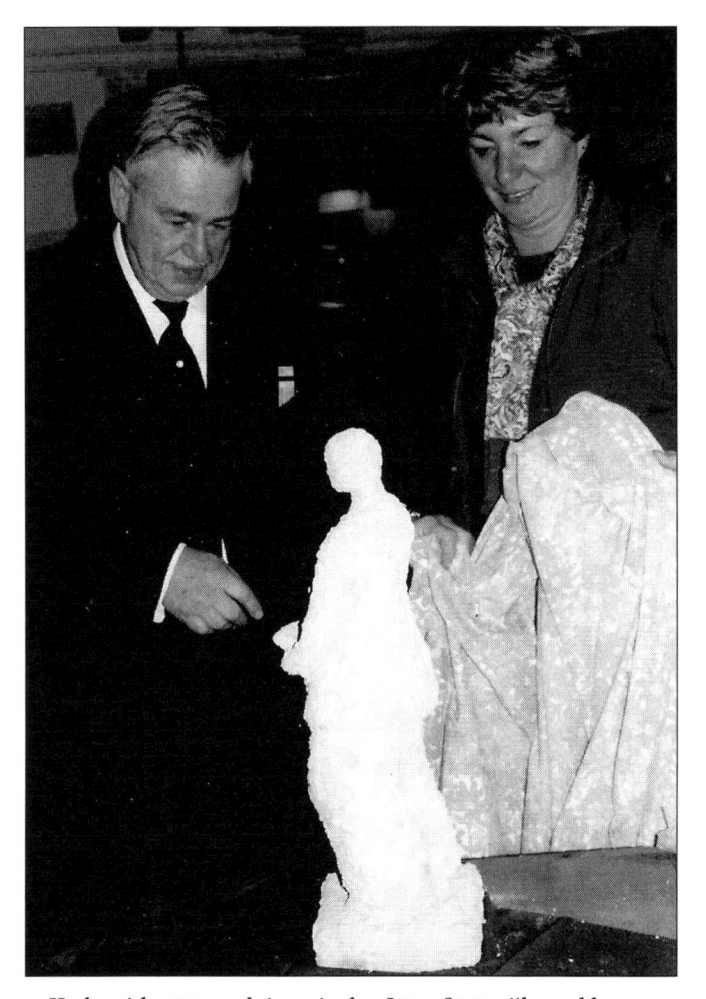

Harky with statue and sister-in-law Lena, Steenwijkerwold, 2003

Harky has decided to donate his body to research after his death. His children know this, and especially his son finds it difficult. A funeral service with an empty casket? Harky thinks that having a sculpture that Annelies's sister has made of him should stand in the church instead. He has already decided the contents of his funeral service. In answering the question of what he would like to do before he dies, Harky does not have to think long. "Keep on doing what I am doing. Spread the dream. Give lectures, do presentations, write articles and do workshops on nonviolent social change through nonviolent means."

Lesbos

In 2016 Harky went to Lesbos (Greece) and reported on the circumstances in which the refugees found themselves. At that time, the general public knew little about their plight. Harky's work on Lesbos included dealing with problems such as discrimination, poverty, violence, and the environment. Harky saw discrimination by some of the local inhabitants and by the authorities who determined whether the refugees would receive residence permits. He saw poverty among the local people who missed the expected income from tourists. There was violence against refugees by the authorities who managed the camps, during deportations, and sometimes by the local people. Questions on the poor conditions in the camps existed then and still exist. Harky tries to bring these problems to the attention of the greater public and so influence politics. Again, he is the press agent.

Life jacket cemetery Lesbos, Greece, 2016

If Harky reviews the situation in the world, he thinks that it might be more worrisome than it was earlier in his life. But he is experienced enough to know that everything happens in waves. Harky says, "True, it is a long road to peace, but I believe that, with God's help, I have changed the world a little bit."

Harky's Dreams of the future

"Out of the spirit of Love, I will continue to work, with the help of God and others, to make the Dream a world-wide reality."

"I hope that you too will join with me so that we can speed up the day when all over the globe will we be able to sing, "We Have Overcome!"

We will be able to sing We have overcome when:

Billions will be given for the prevention of war in place of weapons. And there will be millions of nonviolent peace workers in place of soldiers with guns op their backs.

When setting up field hospitals takes precedence over dropping bombs.

The borders of all lands are open to all.

Our government is more concerned about the safety of the people above the ground than the revenue under the ground.

Trade agreements are made to fill the bellies of the poor and not the wallets of the rich.

Pharmaceutical companies will seek how they can enhance the health of the poorest instead of the stockholders.

The judicial systems will be aimed more at restoration of relationships and less at punishment of offenders.

Freedom of press and art is axiomatic and taken for granted.

People will vote for political parties who want to include all instead of excluding many.

The development of all people, regardless of their sex, race or origin, is promoted instead of being hindered by the abuse of religions and ideologies.

Finally: We will be able to sing We have overcome when:

People treat each other with respect and in Love

Nations will never again go to war,

never prepare for battle again.

Everyone will live in peace

among their own vineyards and fig trees,

and no one will make them afraid.

You Can Kill the Dreamer, but Not the Dream

To the reader

Harky likes to remind people that we cannot all be Dr. Martin Luther King Jr., but we can all be Rosa Parks. Her decision not to give up her seat for a white person was the motivation for Martin Luther King to organize the first protest march. Without Rosa Parks, we would never have heard of Martin Luther King.

"Without Martin Luther King, I would not have dedicated my life to spreading his message, and would this book not have been written."

"A small deed of nonviolence can have great consequences and change the world for the better.

Be the dream
Live the dream
Spread the dream

Then the world will know that the Dreamer has been killed, but not the Dream."

Words of thanks

On the Dutch side of the Atlantic:

THIS ENGLISH VERSION WOULD not have seen daylight was it not that Mrs. Katrien Ruitenburg had previously written the Dutch version. For over seven years, she interviewed me, examined my archives and talked to many family members, relatives and friends. She gave me permission to edit the Dutch version to make it suitable for the American and broader English-speaking public.

Katrien, thanks for having faith in me to do justice to your book.

To all my family and friends, thanks for your time to be interviewed by Katrien and for the written words as they appear in this book.

I want to thank the people who allowed me to use photos, poems and quotations.

I also thank my Dutch publisher, Narratio, for giving me the copy free rights to edit the book for English speakers.

Many thanks go the Mrs. Betty Lavooy for translating the Dutch book into English.

When the English version was ready our friend Richard Knol was very helpful in preparing the book according to the guides of the American publisher, thanks Richard.

On the American side of the Atlantic:

Special thank is in place for my friends Rev. Andrew J. Young, who was willing to write the foreword for the book.

My friend Dr. Sally Harris helped me to edit the English translation, making changes to fit the American idiom and the expectations of the readers outside the Netherlands.

I am very thankful for the time the publishers, Wipf and Stock, have given me to get the English book ready for publication. Without the advice, support, and trust of the staff this book would not be here.

Finally, and most important, I give grateful thanks to my loving wife, Annelies. Without her support, perseverance and knowledge this book not be in your hands.

Harcourt Klinefelter
2019.

Appendix A
Principles of Nonviolence

DR. MARTIN LUTHER KING memorably said, "We have a power that is greater than an atomic bomb. A bomb can only destroy, but nonviolence can change the hearts of people." He also said of his Civil Rights Movement, that he used "the Spirit of Jesus and the techniques of Gandhi."

Gandhi was the first to apply nonviolent protest principles and tactics on a large scale. Since then, there have been large-scale experiments in nonviolent alternatives to war, violence and oppression: the Civil Rights Movement, the Anti-Apartheid struggle, tearing down the Berlin Wall and the vanishing of the Iron Curtain.

This appendix briefly outlines my understanding (given my background in theology, philosophy, psychology and the spirituality of the movements), of the principles of nonviolent social change as articulated and lived by King and Gandhi.

It is not my intention to make an exhaustive list of all the possible principles nor to go into detail and work them out. That would require to much space for this book. Gene Sharp in *The Politics of Nonviolent Action*, lists 198 methods of nonviolent action.

The drawings are from the blackboard in my nonviolence courses as memory aids.

Appendix A—Principles of Nonviolence

Some of the basic principles

Life attitude

Nonviolence is more than simply refusing to use violence. It is choosing to use an alternative: that is, to use positive forces to address violence conflicts and struggle against injustice and oppression. One can adopt a thoroughly nonviolent lifestyle such as a Buddhist monk does. However, it is not necessary to have such a lifestyle in order to use the techniques of nonviolent protest. For instance, anyone can take part in strikes or protest marches.

Life attitudes however are essential since they guide our choices in our lives. If we think that making money is all that matters then we tend to forget that there are immaterial values, such as compassion, concern for other and that love makes for a better world.

Ends and means

One of the most important principles is the relation between ends and means. They should be consonant. Nonviolent alternatives do not say the ends justifies the means. Instead we maintain that the means used must be in keeping with the ends. We should be able to see in the actions taken what ends are envisioned. The means are the seeds of the ends.

As the saying goes: What is the way to get peace? There is no way to peace, peace is the way.

We need to think not just about tomorrow, but also about the day after tomorrow.

Therefore, we need to think ahead of time what steps we need to take to make certain that tomorrow reflects the ends we want.

Appendix A—Principles of Nonviolence

Free will

There must be no coercion in any way. There must be no psychological pressure. At every step of the way a person for whatever reason must feel free not to participate. Even in a sit-in you have the right to leave at the last moment when the police are coming.

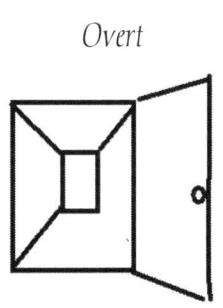

Overt

Whatever we do we accept the consequences of our actions. If we break a law in accordance of our commitment to a higher law we accept the possible punishment of lower law.

Appendix A—Principles of Nonviolence

Satyagraha

This is Gandhi's term for the active attitude of a nonviolent way of life.

Ideally, nonviolence is a way of life that intends to solve conflicts through peaceful means. It is not a passive attitude. On the contrary, it is an active attitude and stance which calls for courage, perseverance and action. In contrast, passivity (not doing anything) is correctly seen as cowardly or ineffective. At best, mere passivity means that there is one less violent person on the planet. But that person will not be an agent of change.

The three aspects of Satyagraha are:

1. Do not use (physical) violence

Do not intentionally kill or injure people.

It is important to recognize that refusing to use violence is based on love and is not as an absolutely abstract commandment, for instance "Thou shall not kill".

Turning the other cheek

Turning the other cheek is not only difficult to put into practice; it is also one of the most misunderstood concepts in the Bible. Many think that "turning the other cheek" is an encouragement to let others "walk all over

Appendix A—Principles of Nonviolence

you." Jesus is not suggesting either that you just submit to violence or "just walk away."

Walking away does not cause the hostile attitude to escalate, but also does not solve the conflict.

In coming back, but without striking back, you make certain points clear:

You are not a coward. It requires courage to return.

You indicate that physical tactics do not scare you, but stimulate you to come back to work on a solution.

You want to keep respect and communication open and mutual. By walking away, all possibility of communication has been broken. By hitting back, you disrupt the communication process.

Coming back implies that you have not written the person off. You say that you appreciate the person, but disapprove of his or her actions

Your intent is to break through the vicious circle of hatred, fear and enmity by replacing enmity with love.

An example:

James Bevel was one of Dr. King's fellow workers. During the time of segregation, he went to a restaurant with a white woman. They were not served. After some time, a man came to him and said, "Nigger, get out of here!" The man hit him, and Bevel fell onto the floor. The man returned to his table. Bevel stood up and went to the man. He said, "Sir, I would like to speak with you." The man hit him again, and Bevel again fell onto the floor.

Bevel then said, "Sir, now that you have proved to everyone here that you are stronger than I am, I would like to speak to you in private." The man was so surprised that he began to talk to Bevel.

In this way Bevel broke down the wall of prejudice in the mind of the attacker.

2. Engage in a joint search for the truth

Gandhi said that nobody has a monopoly on the truth.

The well-known Indian fable of the blind men and the elephant illustrates what Gandhi meant.

Appendix A—Principles of Nonviolence

There were six blind men. None of them had ever seen an elephant. "An elephant", they said, "I wonder what an elephant looks like?"

They went separately to find it out. The first held the elephant by the trunk. The second by a tusk. The third by an ear. The forth by a leg and the fifth by the belly. The sixth by the tail. Then they went home and everyone was convinced that he knew what an elephant looked like.

They began to tell each other. "Oh what is an elephant fantastic", said the first, "so slow and soft, long and strong," "No", said the person who had felt the tusk, "it is somewhat short and very hard." You are both mistaken", said the third, who had felt the ear, "The elephant is flat an thin as big leaf." "Oh no", said the forth who had felt a leg, "He is just like a tree." And the other two said, "He is just like a wall." "He is just like a rope." They argued and argued, and they got angrier and angrier and they began to fight.

Then someone came who could see and said. 'You are all right." he said, "All the parts together are the elephant"

Avoid either or thinking

Another principle in the ongoing search for "truth" is avoid either or thinking that over-simplifies dilemmas. For example, "Either you fight against injustice or you surrender."

APPENDIX A—PRINCIPLES OF NONVIOLENCE

If you keep thinking in black and white terms, you don't see nuances in the gray zones.

You also miss the chance to see all the beautiful colors in the rainbow of alternatives.

3. Soul Power

This is the use of spiritual power to combat physical power.

Basic to this is being "firm in your shoes," radiating self-confidence and fearlessness. A person with soul power stands his/her ground like a block of stone. It is the inspiring power of King's "I have a Dream" speech. Soul power made it possible for the man with suitcases in his hands to stop the tank on the square in Beijing during the Chinese student uprising.

It is what gave martyrs in all ages the strength to chose death rather than give up their beliefs. We saw it in movements such as to gain the right to vote for women and in the Civil Rights actions. Now we see this in the courage of the persons who speak out in the *Me Too* and *LHBTQ* social movements.

It was seen in the Flower Power movement in the Hippie Era.

The Saint Martin's Cross

This is a symbol which consists of a mirror with cross hairs on it surrounded by flowers. The symbol was first used as the basis of an Easter Sunrise service Harky held in front of the Capital of Georgia in Atlanta as part of a vigil commemoration the first anniversary of the assassination of Dr. Martin Luther King, Jr.

Appendix A—Principles of Nonviolence

The story behind it is as follows. Jesus was crucified on a cross of wood. St. Peter upside down and St. St. Andrew diagonally. Many of the saints are symbolized by their martyrdom. My pastor, Dr. Martin Luther King, Jr., was crucified on the sight of a sniper's rifle. Hence the cross hairs. Jesus said if you want to be my disciple you must deny yourself and pick up your cross. To be his disciple in this day and age you may have to lead such a life that you too are in some snipers sights. This is the way our age stones its prophets. Hence the mirror. As a friend of mine and Dr. King said, "That is too horrible to think about. Yet that is what the cross meant originally. It was the teargas, the billy club and the gun of the day. This was the way the state got rid of dissent. Yet the church took this symbol of oppression and death and transformed it into the symbol of life. Today the flower symbolizes new of life.

Love

Love is very important, not only for the victims, but also for the perpetrators. One should put the words of Jesus into action: "Love your enemy."

At the funeral for the four children who were killed when the Klu Klux Klan blew up their church in Birmingham, Alabama, Martin Luther King said, "Probably no exhortation from Jesus is more difficult to follow than the command to love your enemy." The basis for the love for your enemy is that even your enemy is the object of the love of the Creator. It will grieve the Creator if you harm the object of His love.

Appendix A — Principles of Nonviolence

I remember a peace demonstration where a vicious racist taunted the defenseless people with vile language. Someone then said to me and also audibly to others, "Do not forget that this man was also someone for whom Jesus died." Then he left the safety of the group and went to the racist and tried to talk to him, a courageous action on his part.

Looking at this principle, we must refuse to reward evil with evil.

Dr. King said, "When you rise to love on this level, you love all men not because you like them, not because their ways appeal to you, but you love them because God loves them. This is what Jesus meant when he said, 'Love your enemies.' And I'm happy that he didn't say, 'Like your enemies' because there are some people that I find it pretty difficult to like."

You don't have to like a person to be concerned about his/her well being.

Appendix A—Principles of Nonviolence

Moral Judo

In the second chapter of the book *The Power of Non-Violence* by Richard B. Gregg, he used the used the term "Moral Jiu-tsu" to describe the psychological mechanism of nonviolence by relating it to the physical mechanism used in martial arts.

I prefer to use judo as an example describing this physical and moral force.

In most fighting sports there is a direct, head on class of forces.

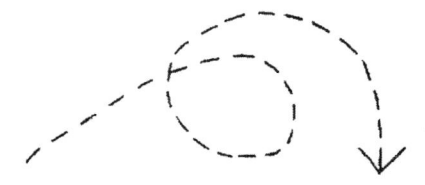

In judo it is different. You use the opponent's own strength to reach your goal. Instead of going head on against the attacker, you use the momentum of the attacker's charge to help go in the direction he or she is going but then with an unexpected twist.

Thus, even at the physical level, it is not always true that the strongest wins. Not only can this principle of judo work on the physical level, it can also be used on the mental or spiritual level.

Instead of directly going against the negative arguments of the opponent, you look for something positive in his or her arguments/values that you can use for your purposes. You reinforce the positive aspects, especially the moral awareness. In this way on the mental level you bring him or her out balance and use this moral momentum to help him or her go in an different direction.

A personal example:

Appendix A — Principles of Nonviolence

Pistol packing mama

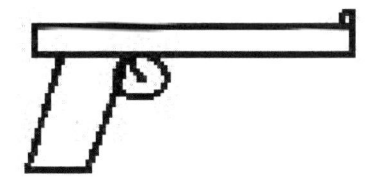

In preparation for one of King's speeches, a colleague and I were busy testing a sound car in a park when suddenly a middle-aged man came running over the field and hid behind a tree. After him came an angry woman with a pistol. If the woman moved one way the man behind the tree moved in the other direction so as to keep the tree trunk between him and the woman. Hosea Williams, a member of Dr. King's staff, picked up the microphone and called out, "Madam, think about your children! I can imagine that your man did something horrible. Otherwise you would not want to shoot him. But think about your children. If you shoot and kill your husband, then they will no longer have a father. They will put you in jail. Then they will also have no mother in their home. What will happen to them? Think about them." It was not long before she gave her pistol to Hosea. Afterwards Williams mediated the family quarrel with success.

Williams made an appeal to a positive value he suspected the woman had—motherly love. He helped her see the consequences of what would happen if she carried out her negative and violent revenge plan.

Not only adults but also children have a moral awareness. Two anecdotes in Chapter 8, about an ice cream cone and a snowman, are examples of this.

Moral Judo can also be used on a group level:

Appendix A—Principles of Nonviolence

The Playground

In the sixties there was a demonstration for the preservation of a playground built by local residents. According to the police, there were demonstrators who threw stones at them. The police shot and killed one person and injured several onlookers. The leadership of the movement was confronted with a dilemma. If they marched the next day, there would be the danger that the people who were angry at the police would use violence. Then there was the chance that more people would be killed. Calling off the demonstration, though, would not only take the momentum out of the struggle, but also confirm once more that violence has the last word. What would you do if you were the leader?

The march was held the next day. People demonstrated not only for the preservation of the playground, but also against the excessive police violence. There was no violence from either side. The reason? Everyone in the march had their hands tied behind their backs. The police had no reason to use force. If they did, they knew they would look ridiculous.

The "Human carpet." described in Chapter 5 is another example of appealing to the conscience of the people in place of physically trying to stop them.

Here ends the listing of the basic principles. I now want to explore some of the obstacles to applications of these principles in general.

Appendix A—Principles of Nonviolence

You can't expect people to choose for nonviolent means if they know very little about it.

Not only has Dr. King' method of nonviolent social change been marginalized, people do not really get the chance to hear about nonviolent victories.

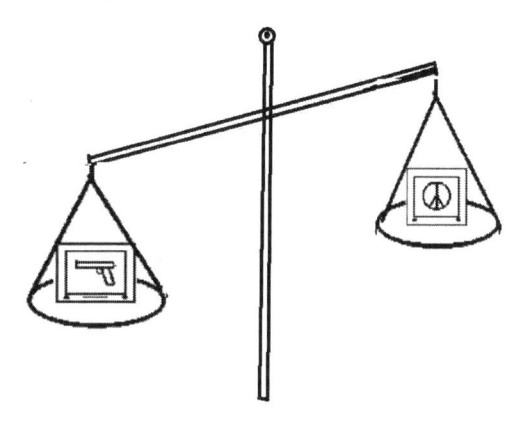

How many war films have you seen?

How many television programs have you watched in which the police resolve criminal acts with violence?

Now ask your self how many films have you seen in which there is a nonviolent solution to either a personal or social problems?

How much have you learned in history classes about nonviolent victories?

In the past mostly white males have written the schoolbooks and we only learn how the use of violence has solved all the social problems. The winners are always the good guys (Cowboy mentality).

One way we might implement a culture of peace and nonviolence is by demanding equal time for nonviolent heroes and actions in the media, in schools programs and history books.

To institute peace education in the schools and teach students *peer mediation* is a step in the direction of learning about nonviolent ways to deal with conflicts. To help students (and grown-ups) understand where racism and discrimination, oppression and keeping the other "in its place" come from and how oppressive institutions work, is by making space for finding nonviolent solutions to deal with these problems. Dealing with bullying is in many schools a central theme and fortunately some good nonviolent programs have been developed to help students experience what it does to a person who is bullied and the one who is bullying. These programs also work in situations where it concerns adults, for example on the work floor.

Trainings in nonviolence on all the topics mentioned above will help people to decide how they will deal with a conflict or violent situation.

Once people understand the mechanisms about creative nonviolence they are usually able to adept this creativity in many life situations for the benefit for peace and justice.

Lack of funds for peaceful social change

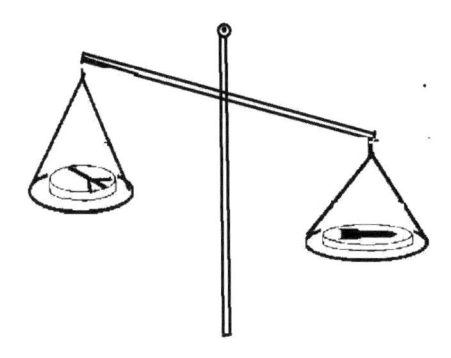

Compare how much money governments spend for the prevention of war to what is spent on weapons.

Needless to say if we use even a fraction of what we spend on violent defense we could provide much more constructive social services and better education and health care. But is doesn't happen. Ask yourself why? The answer is simple.

You give peace away. You sell weapons. There are no profits in prophets. The military industrial complex that President Eisenhower warned us about is very much alive.

These remarks apply to government spending. It is another question whether non-government agencies like Peace Brigades International, Christian Peacemakers Teams, etc. should accept governmental funding or remain independent from indirect governmental control.

Appendix A—Principles of Nonviolence

We tried nonviolence but it didn't work.

Sometimes we hear from action groups words to this effect: "We tried nonviolence, but it didn't work. Therefore, we gave up on nonviolence and have gone over to violent tactics."

The problem may have been not that nonviolence didn't work but that the tactics were not nonviolent enough. Many think that they can effectively stop some injustice overnight just by holding a big march or a boycott without having a well thought out long-term strategy and campaign as well as training. What would be the chances of winning a battle if the soldiers had no training or the leaders had no strategy?

A nonviolent struggle can fail by not being nonviolent enough.

It is imperative that the demonstrators not use violence. Therefore it is of the greatest importance that steps are taken to prevent violence on the part of your own people. If violence erupts from out of your own group, it gives an excuse for the police or other authorities to use more violence on their part. The danger is that your group will lose public sympathy.

Because violence is so toxic, sometimes the other side sends in infiltrators, *agents provocateurs*, as to provoke violence. They often use radical language and encourage people to use violence as a necessary tactic. They sound like well-meaning radicals, but they disappear when the police start to come. Often they are part of a splinter group that, somewhere else, starts throwing stones or "trashing store windows."

Whether those who want the march to use violence are well meaning radicals who believe that violence is necessary to win the cause, like Mao who said, "Political power comes out the barrel of a gun" or agents provocateurs, we treat them in the same way. There are nonviolent means to counter their actions. The Portuguese Bull Fight (See Chapter 5) is a technique that was first used in nonviolent demonstrations in America and I adapted it for use in psychiatric institutions.

There is another factor which can lead to violence in one own ranks.

That is the situation that arises when someone tries to defend a person who is the victim of an attacker.

The usual response to try to protect a victim from a physical attract is to attack the attacker. The problem is that the defender actions usually

Appendix A—Principles of Nonviolence

invoke a response from the friends of the attacker. They then try to help their friend and my friends will the join in and in the shortest time we will have a riot. That is the last thing that we want.

Dr. King said, "You have to fight in such a way that you can live with your enemy after the fight is over." We put this into practice in demonstrations.

When someone was being attacked we were not passive or looked the other way. We took action. We did not attack the attacker.

Instead we threw our bodies over the person being attacked. Thereby protecting the victim as well as not injuring the attacker. Nonviolence is not for cowards (See Chapter 4 how this tactic saved the life of Rev Andrew Young headings "Demonstrations against the war in Vietnam").

In conclusion.

I present the following diagram to highlight the different aspects mentioned in the above texts.

A picture is worth a thousand words.

Appendix A—Principles of Nonviolence

Diagram of Alternatives to Violence

2 PERSON SITUATION

FIGHT BACK

RUN AWAY

TURN OTHER CHEEK

3 PERSON SITUATION

Pax Romana = attack aggressor
Protection of te victim by using violence

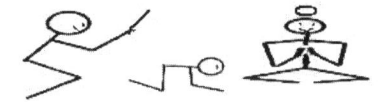

Pax Pilati = hands washing in innocence
looking away from the victim, doing nothing
The victim remains unprotected;

Pax Christi = protecting the victim without violence
protecting the victim by incarcerating self the violence

Appendix B
Résumé

Personal

Name: Harcourt (Harky) Klinefelter
Address: Blaankamp 15
Town: Steenwijkerwold, the Netherlands
Postcode: 8341 PA
Telephone : + 31 (0)521-588553
E-mail: pluspunt@antenna.nl
www.harcourt-klinefelter.org
Nationality: Dutch and American
Date of birth: 2 March, 1938
Civil status: Married, 3 children

Education

1959-1963:
Bachelor of Arts in Philosophy (cum laude), Bloomfield College, Bloomfield, New Jersey, U.S.A.
1963-1968:
Master of Divinity, Yale Divinity School, Yale University. Thesis: *"The Church as a Movement rather than an Institution."* New Haven, Connecticut, U.S.A.

Appendix B—Résumé

Professional Life

1969.
Ordained in the United Church of Christ, USA
1989:
Ordained in the Mennonite Church, the Netherlands

Work Experiences

1965-1969:
Assistant Director Public Relations for Dr. Martin Luther King's organization, The Southern Christian Leadership Conference (S.C.L.C.), Atlanta, Georgia.
1969-1972:
Ministry to the Street People: work with the hippies, Atlanta, Georgia.
1972-1974:
factory worker: Philips Drachten, the Netherlands
1974-1986:
Volkshogeschool Overcinge: course leader in a residential adult education center. Specialty: initiator and coordinator of the project, "Peace and a More Just Society." Havelte, the Netherlands
1989-1994:
Minister in the Mennonite Church, (Doopsgezinde Gemeente), Zeist, the Netherlands
1994-1998:
Head trainer for the Pluspunt Foundation: "Conflict Mediation and Conflict Prevention, trainings in the refugee centers with staff and refugees", the Netherlands
1995—1996:
European consultant and trainer for CSIS (Center for Strategic and International Studies), Washington DC, "Training in Conflict Resolution for Church Representatives in Serbia, Croatia and Bosnia".
1996—present:
Speaking engagements and trainings in the Netherlands, around Europe and USA

Appendix B—Résumé
International activities

1972:
World Council of Churches Consultation "Violence, Nonviolence and Social Justice" Cardiff, Wales

1974:
World Council of Churches Consultation, "Nonviolence and Communes." Geneva, Switzerland.

1977:
Nonviolence training, Sweden

1978:
Participant upon invitation in the Conference of peace researchers and trainers "Disarmament and Conversion Strategies for Small Nations" Oslo, Norway

1978 and 1983:
Nonviolence trainings, University de la Paix, Belgium

1980:
Nonviolence training, Denmark

1983:
Resource Person at a UNESCO-sponsored conference on nonviolence in the Interuniversity Center, Dubrovnik, Yugoslavia

1993–present:
Training and support of refugees and other war victims, Croatia and Bosnia

1993–present:
Conferences of trainers in nonviolent conflict resolution in Europe

2007-2013:
Board member of Church and Peace, Germany

2015:
SCLC-SCOPE 50th Anniversary Reunion. Workshop leader in nonviolence, Atlanta, Georgia

2016:
CPT(Christian Peacemaker Teams), work with refugees, Lesbos, Greece

2018:
Lectures at the University of Texas and nonviolence trainings, El Paso, Texas

Appendix B—Résumé

Publications

2018
Book:
"Het leven van vredesapostel Harcourt Klinefelter, Globalisering van de droom van Dr. Martin Luther King", (The Life of Peace Apostle Harcourt Klinefelter, Globalizing the Dream of Dr. Martin Luther King) by Katrien Ruitenburg, 2018, Narratio; ISBN 978 90 5263 9383.

Articles

Over the years many articles have appeared in local, national and international newspapers and magazines.

Articles in Books

1999
Dr. Martin Luther King, Gidsen en getuigen op de pilgrimage naar vrede, (Guides and Witnesses on the Pilgrimage to Peace), Paul van Dijk, Herman Noordgraaf and Greetje Witte-Rang, editors, pages 183-194, 1999, Narratio, ISBN 978905 2 631868

2003
"Strategieën voor een andere wereld?",(Strategies for an Other World) in *In eigen boezem,* (A search into the source of violence in the Christian tradition), Cees den Heyer and Sjon Donkers, editors, 2003, Narratio, ISBN 978905 2 63984

2009
Oorlog verkopen: over taal, media, religion en propaganda (Selling war, language, media, religion, propaganda) , Ton van der Lingen, Greetje Witte-rang, editors, 2009, Narratio, ISBN 978905 2 2636511

Public Speeches:

Over the years many speeches were held in schools, universities, churches, clubs and special events.

For over 25 years speeches held at the Dr. Martin Luther King, Jr. Tribute and Dinner, Wassenaar, the Netherlands. Sponsored by OAR, *Overseas Americans Remember.*

Appendix B — Résumé

February 15, 2003
Demonstration Against the New War, Amsterdam, the Netherlands
January 26, 2008
Globalising the Dream Of Dr. Martin Luther King Jr. Heidelberg, Germany
May 5, 2013 and 2016
Bevrijdingsfestival (Liberation Festival),
Zwolle and Assen, the Netherlands
April 2017
Opening speech: "The American Dream", Drents Museum, Assen, the Netherlands
January 15, 2019
National Celebration of the 90 Birthday of Martin Luther King keynote speaker, Almere, the Netherlands

Television :

Over the years many appearance in talk shows.
April 2, 2018 Documentary: "In de schaduw van King",(In the Shadow of King) 1 hour , national Dutch broadcast
Internet: "Sunday Morning Blues" 10 min. film about relation to Dr. M.L. King, Geschiedenis TV(History TV)
Internet: Greenpeace Netherland "De kracht van geweldloos protest (The power of nonviolent protest) 5:14 min.

Hobbies

birdwatching
guitar playing
skating
traveling

Appendix C
Photo and poem credits

Cover

Photographer: Mirajm Lensink
www.lens-inc.nl <http://www.lens-inc.nl/> -
Mirjam@lens-inc.nl <mailto: Mirjam@lens-inc.nl>

Foreword

Photo Andrew Young
Photographer: J.D. Scott
Copy right: Â © 2013 J.D. Scott Photography, Inc.
November 26, 2013

Chapter 2

Hymn: "Just as I am" by Charlotte Elliot, (1789-1871), 1836

Litany: "The Coventry Litany of Reconciliation"
Copyright@2019 The Community of the Cross of Nails
The community has given permission to use this text in the book of Klinefelter

Appendix C — Photo and poem credits

Chapter 3

Photo Harky and King 1966
Photographer Bob Fitch gave personal permission to use this photo.

Photo "Joan Baez leads singing, annual Southern Christian Leadership Conference staff workshop Penn Center, Frogmore, South Carolina, 1966" SourceID: M1994_MLK__0250_Frogmore_841_24
Bob Fitch Photography Archive, Special Collections Department, Stanford University Library.
Stanford University is happy to offer you a non-exclusive offer license to reproduce an image from the Bob Fitch archive.

Chapter 4

Photo Hosea Williams, Carl Zitlow, Harky and Thea Lucia
Photographer: Brig Cabe (deceased)

Chapter 5

Photo Daddy King, Harky, and Rev. Gray
Photographer: Brig Cabe (deceased)

Chapter 8

Poem: "Love"
(anonymous), in Masterpieces of Religious Verse,
James Dalton Morrison, ed.,
New York: Harper, 1948

Chapter 9

Photo Action at the Johannes Post army base,
Havelterberg Drenthe, the Netherlands
Groningen Press Monday, May 30 1988.
Photographer: Sake Elzinga
Sake Elzinga Photography
sake@xs4all.nl

APPENDIX C—PHOTO AND POEM CREDITS

Photo Harky with hat
Mirjam Lensink
www.lens-inc.nl <http://www.lens-inc.nl/> -
Mirjam@lens-inc.nl <mailto: Mirjam@lens-inc.nl.>

Appendix A

Principles of Nonviolence

The Politics of Nonviolent Action by Gene Sharp, Porter Sargent, USA, 1972,

The Power of Non-Violence by Richard B. Gregg, Narvajivan Publishing House, Ahmadabad, India, 1938

Printed in Poland
by Amazon Fulfillment
Poland Sp. z o.o., Wrocław